Adulting for Christians

Adulting
for Christians

An Interactive Guide to Keeping the
Faith While Learning the Ropes

Jenny Ingram

ROCKRIDGE
PRESS

Interior and Cover Designer: Eric Pratt
Art Producer: Karen Williams
Editor: Morgan Shanahan

Title page: Illustration by Niki Fisher

Copyright page: Illustration © 2020 Niki Fisher.
Author photo courtesy of © Brittany Kelley

ISBN: 978-1-64611-442-9

R0

I dedicate this book to my "kids," Joel, Livi & Lucy. Aaaaaand to so many of my other kids who have come through our front door, stayed up all night talking/gaming WAY too loud in the basement, consumed tons of junk food at the kitchen counter, and been given countless hugs & so many pieces of my mama's heart. These words have been written in prayer and with hope for your success, happiness, and ongoing faith. You are deeply loved and I am so excited to cheer you on as you take on some of your most cool, confusing, sweet, and life-defining years. Finally, wise words from Judith from the movie Gentlemen Broncos, *"Remember who you are and what you stand for!"*

Contents

Introduction

Welcome to ADULTING! Welcome to the land of responsibility! Welcome to bills and bosses and grocery shopping and meal planning (YAWN) and . . . total freedom to decide when to (or not to) go to bed! As a fully fledged adulting adult, I'd say one of the BIGGEST perks of adulthood is the **freedom**.

It is likely the most intimidating part of adulting, too.

I've crossed my fair share of decades and I'm going to be honest—turning twenty was *the actual worst.*

I wept.

Turning twenty felt like I had to turn my back on roller skates and lemonade stands. I didn't realize until it was too late that childhood was . . . a pretty sweet gig. I spent a good part of my childhood working so hard to grow up, then at nineteen I realized I wanted a rewind. Or at least a *hard stop.* The adult-level freedom felt like a freight train charging at me loaded with shipping containers full of unknowns.

Oh, but we have hope and we have comfort! As it says in 1 Peter 5:7, **"Casting all your care upon him; for He careth for you."**

There I was, squandering the first of my adulting moments stuck in fear despite biblical promise after promise after promise of companionship and care. What is the opposite of freedom? *Probably worry.* Such a waste of time!

The Bible is bursting with words of hope. "I sought the Lord, and He heard me, and delivered me from all my fears" (Psalms 34:4). Don't do what I did. Don't waste one minute of your good health, sharp mind, and youthful energy and complexion on worry! God's word is filled with promises and reminders that you've got this, baby, and more importantly—this is not your path to brave all alone.

What are you waiting for? *Let's do this!*

"So whether you eat or drink or whatever you do, do it all for the glory of God."

–1 Corinthians 10:31

Chapter One

The Practical Stuff

Finding a Suitable Place to Adult

So. You're ready. You grew out of that twin-size bed yeeeeears ago, and though home-cooked meals are fantastic and all...
it's time.

What stands between you and moving to a place of your own? Asking yourself some questions can help with your preparation:

- Rent or buy? The chances are higher now than ever that renting is your only choice, so we are going to dig a bit deeper into that option.

- Can I afford something on my own, or do I need a roomie (or two or three or four)?

- *Where* do I want to live? Are there bars on the windows? Will Uber Eats deliver to that location?

- Do I have enough saved to cover the setup costs? Wait, *what setup costs*? Will you need a bed and pots and pans? You'll definitely need enough cash for the first month's rent, last month's rent, and a chunk for security deposit as well. See the checklist that follows for more on all of that up-front cost fun.

Apartment Hunting Checklist

☐ What is your budget? _____

☐ What is your credit score? _____ Know what your
landlord requires, and know what your score is. (To learn
more about credit scores and how they work check out
page 149.)

☐ Gather references (two to three), proof of employment, and
bonus points by drafting a letter expressing what an ideal
tenant you will be. List two trusted potential references
here (not your mom): _____

☐ Prepare for up-front costs: first and last month's rent,
cleaning deposit, utilities, Internet, parking, renters insurance, and pet deposit. How much do you currently have
saved? _____

☐ Read that lease agreement. Ask questions before signing.
(When is the rent due? Do you need to mow? What if the
oven breaks? Nails to hang art or adhesive strips?) What
maintenance/upkeep is your responsibility? Drop a couple
other questions you might have here: _____

_____

_____

_____

_____

_____

_____

☐ Pray. A little prayer never hurt anyone—am I right?

"For I know the thoughts that I think toward you, saith the Lord, thoughts of peace, and not of evil, to give you an expected end."

—*Jeremiah 29:11*

Basically? God's got your back. He has serious plans for your prosperity, hope, and future. Speaking of hopes . . . what are yours?

_____

_____

_____

_____

_____

_____

_____

_____

_____

_____

_____

_____

_____

_____

_____

_____

_____

_____

Maintenance and Insurance: The Secret to Having Nice Things

Until now, it is probable you have lived a life free of domestic-type maintenance. Have you ever cleaned an oven, replaced an air filter, or changed the batteries in a smoke alarm? Speaking of alarms . . . property insurance anyone?

The insurance struggle is *real*. Considering options and what types of insurance you'll actually *need* can be overwhelming, but you've done hard things! The essentials are auto, property (home or renters), health, and life insurance. Do you own anything unique, like antiques or jewelry, that might be worth protecting as well? (This usually includes things like engagement rings or family heirlooms.)

Other insurances to consider (some depend on region): earthquake, flood, pet (we love our fur babies!), disability (waving to the self-employed), and catastrophic insurance if you just can't financially swing full-on health insurance just yet.

Insurance Vocab Matching Game!

Do you know how to read your insurance policy? Let's find out!
Draw a line to connect the jargon to its correct definition.

Deductible

An account that lets you save for future medical costs.

Out-of-pocket

Approval for care by insurance company. Because they think they know better than your physician, apparently.

Preauthorization

A fixed amount to be paid to provider at time of service.

Co-pay

Regular payments made to insurance to maintain coverage

Premium

Amount you pay to your care provider at each visit before insurance benefits kick in (when this amount is higher, the overall cost of the plan tends to be lower)

Health savings account

Costs to be paid by you/your wallet, above the premium amount

*Answer key

Deductible *Amount you pay to your care provider at each visit before insurance benefits kick in (when this amount is higher, the overall cost of the plan tends to be lower)*

Out-of-pocket *Costs to be paid by you/your own wallet, above the premium amount*

Preauthorization *Approval for care by insurance company. Because they think they know better than your physician, apparently.*

Co-pay *A fixed amount to be paid to provider at time of service.*

Premium *Regular payments made to insurance to maintain coverage*

Health savings account *An account that lets you save for future medical costs.*

HSA, *What?*

Why are Health Savings Accounts so awesome? Well, it's a pre-tax (not taxable) savings account. The savings are used to pay for medical bills, which is handy. But even *more* handy are all the other items the account can help pay for, including, but not limited to, dental exams, flu shots, lab fees, contacts, chiropractor visits, select over-the-counter medicines, feminine hygiene products, lice treatments (oh, I pray you avoid that!) . . . and: Every. Single. Doctor.

"Look at the birds of the air, for they neither sow nor reap nor gather into barns; yet your heavenly Father feeds them. Are you not of more value than they?"

—*Matthew 6:26*

Don't freak out. Thinking about alllllllll the reasons you may or may not need insurance might create some anxiety. Break out that Bible. Read through Matthew 6:26–34. Write out the passage in your own words.

_____

_____

_____

_____

_____

_____

_____

_____

_____

_____

_____

_____

_____

_____

Should an item or space be cleaned?

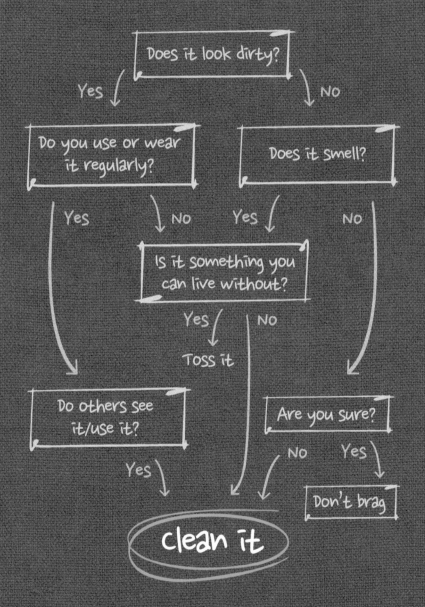

Does it look dirty?

Yes — Do you use or wear it regularly?

No — Does it smell?

Do you use or wear it regularly?
- Yes → Do others see it/use it?
- No → Is it something you can live without?

Does it smell?
- Yes → Is it something you can live without?
- No → Are you sure?

Is it something you can live without?
- Yes → Toss it
- No → clean it

Do others see it/use it?
- Yes → clean it

Are you sure?
- No → clean it
- Yes → Don't brag

clean it

Stuff That Needs Cleaning and How Often It Needs It

Weekly

- *Finger test!* If you don't have a white glove, just use your finger. Slide it across the top of that shelf, table, and TV. Is anything there? Then clean it!

- Wash your bedding (at *least* every other week). Think about it... the sweat, the hair, the shedding of skin all up in those sheet fibers.

- Clean the bathroom (disinfect and scrub the heck out of that sink, toilet, and tub)

- Quick fridge purge (dump old leftovers, take inventory in prep for meal planning)

- Sweep and vacuum (more often if you have kids or pets!)

- Dust (every other week might be OK, unless guests is coming to visit)

- Water your plants

- Doorknobs and handles (wipe them down, because *germs*)

Monthly

- Dust baseboards (Those are the boards between the wall and the floor. Not all places have them, but most do. If you haven't noticed them or the dirt that collects on them before... you will now, and you'll be appalled at the little dust collectors they are!)

- Mop (Spot cleaning helps delay the need to break out the bucket. **Pro tip:** Baby wipes are *fantastic* spot-cleaning tools!)

- Vacuum under cushions

- Wipe down appliances

- Wipe down fronts and little grime-grabbing edges of the kitchen cabinets, too

Quarterly Basics

- Windows

- Oven

- Overachievers: flip mattress

Biannually

- Smoke alarm batteries—I recommend checking the alarm when we "Spring forward" and "fall back"!

True or false?

"Cleanliness is next to godliness" is a Bible verse.

False! *It is often referred to as a verse, but actually, it is a quote from a sermon given by John Wesley in 1778. Phew! That should release a lot of pressure, right?*

*"And whatsoever ye do, do it heartily,
as to the Lord, and not unto men."*

—*Colossians 3:23*

*How might the words in this verse change your attitude
about the drudgery of chores and cleaning?*

_____

_____

_____

_____

_____

_____

_____

_____

_____

_____

_____

_____

_____

_____

_____

_____

_____

Being Prepared When Things Break

Adulting means knowing why we don't throw Frisbees in the house: because adulting means the cost of repair comes from our bank account now, or at least from our security deposit. Refer to your lease agreement to better understand what things you are responsible to fix versus what your landlord is required to take care of.

Are you a unicorn who owns your own home? 'Cause then it's definitely on you to fix. Regardless of whether you rent or own, buy or assemble a tool kit of essentials:

- ☐ Hammer

- ☐ Phillips and flat-head screwdrivers

- ☐ Tape measure

- ☐ Level

- ☐ Nails

- ☐ Wrench

- ☐ Pliers

- ☐ Superglue

- ☐ Utility knife

- ☐ Duct tape

- ☐ Fire extinguisher

Handy-homemaker tool kits abound on Amazon, but I love the one I got at IKEA.

Other important things:

- Know where to shut off the water, at both the water main and at each appliance (toilet/sink/washer)! I can't tell you where your main shut-off valve is, but you can Google search how to do it. You know what? Maybe just put down the book and go do that now. Don't forget that Google is our info-finding bestie.

- Know where your electrical panel is . . . and *what* an electrical panel is.

- Do you have any appliances that use natural gas? Learn how to shut off those valves, too. YouTube is another info-finding bestie!

Do the Lame Stuff First

Seriously. Just get it out of the way, yo.

☐ Pay the parking ticket

☐ Do the dishes (dishes left too long make your home stink—gross!)

☐ Scrub the toilet (*please*)

☐ If you are self-employed . . . keep up on those quarterly taxes (I speak from experience riddled with penalties upon compounded interest penalties.)

Pro tip: If you don't know about how very special and fancy the self-employed tax situation is ... *learn it, friend.* This will surely be one of the *lamest* adulting tasks of all (unless you are a certified public accountant, a.k.a. a CPA), and it is also one of the most *critical* tasks as a self-employed type. Do yourself a favor: Fork over the dough and meet with a CPA (unless you are a CPA). Talk taxes and insurance, too.

> *What do you think keeps you from doing the hard things? Commit Galatians 6:9 to memory as you launch headfirst into adulting and the lame stuff that comes with it ... "And let us not be weary in well doing: for in due season we shall reap, if we faint not."*

"Every prudent man dealeth with knowledge: but a fool layeth open his folly."

—Proverbs 13:16

In other words: Be wise, not foolish. OK?

Chapter Two

Acting Like a Responsible Human

Maintain Your Mental and Physical Health

When you have a broken bone, it's easy to recognize that professional care is needed. Or if you sound like a seal when you cough, it's pretty clear you need professional intervention there, too.

However, when it comes to our mental health, there is often a lack of any clear, physical evidence of a problem. *But hear this*—mental health challenges are just as important to tend to as any open wound! In fact, mental health issues left unchecked can have an even more devastating effect. What might have been somewhat easy to deal with in the beginning can turn over into a lifetime battle in the blink of an eye. Being a proactive advocate for your mental wellness is important and serious.

Issues with mental health and wellness are normal. In fact, they are probably more common than you realize, and if you are in the pit of your own struggle, it can be hard to see that you are not the only one struggling. Don't give fear and shame control over your lifelong mental wellness.

Invest in Your Long-Term Physical Health

When was the last time you visited a doctor?

Be honest. One doesn't have to be sick to see a doctor (this goes for mental health, too). Regular check-ups aren't just for kids. What are reasons you hesitate to visit the doctor regularly? Fear of bad news? Shots? Getting weighed?

Ignorance is not bliss, particularly when ignorance means serious issues go unchecked and become (wait for it . . .) more serious. Related: More serious = more expensive. Also related: All that insurance stuff we talked about on page 5, and knowing what it does and does not cover.

Get yourself set up with a regular doctor. Ask friends and coworkers for their recommendations. Consider a nurse practitioner or naturopath (that's a health practitioner who offers natural remedies). Yay options!

Invest in Your Long-Term Mental Health

Mental wellness can be a significant struggle. Scripture may not solve all our problems, but it is rich with comfort and encouragement. We are reminded over and over in God's word that He has our back. John 11:35 says, "Jesus wept." Jesus wept with Lazarus's family, and He weeps with you. Psalms 34:18 tells us that the Lord is near the brokenhearted and saves the crushed spirit. And in Matthew 11:28 Jesus said, "Come unto me, all you that labor and are heavy laden, and I will give you rest."

Help Him Help You

Yes, scripture offers great promise, but don't under-estimate the benefit of an established relationship with a doctor, counselor, therapist, or pastor, and if you or someone you know needs help, here are some solid resources to start with:

- Text CONNECT to 741741 to text with the Crisis Text Line in the United States

- Visit https://www.faithfulcounseling.com/ to connect with a faith-based therapist online

- Call 1-800-273-8255 for the National Suicide Prevention Lifeline (and, by the way, you can and absolutely should call before you become suicidal)

*"Finally, brethren, whatsoever things
are true, whatsoever things are honest,
whatsoever things are just, whatsoever
things are pure, whatsoever things are lovely,
whatsoever things are of good report; if there
be any virtue, and if there be any praise, think
on these things."*

—*Philippians 4:8*

*List the things in your life that are lovely, good, and
praiseworthy. Read your words out loud in a prayer of
thanksgiving and appreciation. Refer back when you
need to fight those negative thoughts.*

_____

_____

_____

_____

_____

_____

_____

_____

_____

_____

_____

_____

_____

Cooking 101: Feeding Yourself and Others

Keep It Simple: Kitchen Basics

When all else fails, make cereal! Ramen is cool, too—throw in a hard-boiled egg for extra protein. Don't know how to hard-boil an egg? No problem! Trader Joe's sells them in a bag! Beginning adulting is pressure enough. It's okay to have cereal for dinner, just not *every* night. Here are some key recommended items to stock in your kitchen for adequate meal preparation:

- ☐ Big pot (yay, heating up many cans of soup for a party!)
- ☐ Frying pan
- ☐ Spatula
- ☐ Colander
- ☐ Sharp knife (chop those onions!)
- ☐ Forks, spoons, knives
- ☐ Cups, bowls, plates
- ☐ Cutting board
- ☐ A Pyrex dish or two
- ☐ Cookie sheet
- ☐ Meat thermometer
- ☐ Fire extinguisher (Yes, again. Get one.)

Anything else is bonus. With the items above (minus the fire extinguisher) you can prepare a respectable meal.

Master Three Dishes

That's your goal. Just three dishes. Here's one that maximizes versatility as you nourish yourself and possibly some guests:

Chicken Breasts FTW—made from fresh or frozen chicken!

- Heat oven to 350°F.

- Spray a Pyrex dish with cooking spray.

- Place breast(s) on the Pyrex (you do not need to defrost frozen breasts—cool, right?).

- Sprinkle with salt and pepper. If you have some garlic powder, lightly sprinkle on some of that, too.

- Bake for 30 minutes. Use a meat thermometer to make sure internal temp reaches 160°F. A meat thermometer should become one of your besties, but the nonthermometer way to make sure it's cooked adequately is—is there any pink? Cooked chicken should have ZERO pink.

There are lots of serving options/pairings here: top with canned spaghetti sauce and mozzarella, serve with pasta, slice and add to a baked potato, build a sandwich, put on a salad, or enjoy as a late-night protein snack.

Health and Financial Implications of Cooking Your Own Food

Pro tips:

- **Meat:** Cook most meats to 160°F. When in doubt, Google it.

- **Leftover life:** Three to four days

- **Expiration dates:** Pay attention to dates on cans and containers. They're not just suggestions.

- **Take caution:** When in doubt, throw it out.

- **Stay fresh:** Shop the perimeter of the grocery store. Aisles are full of packaged and prepared foods that are generally more expensive and not as good for you.

- **Utilize coupons:** Take advantage and stock up on deals if you have space. If you don't have room for five extra tubes of toothpaste, it's probably for the better to let it go. It's not a good deal if you don't need it.

What are two other dishes you can make, or think you can learn to make? Are there any childhood favorites you'd like to add to your meal-making repertoire? Though boxed meals (mac and cheese) may not be the best, they still count. They are cheaper than fast food, and every penny counts—am I right? Don't forget about Pinterest inspiration!

Entertaining Pro Tip

Sauté some onions (sauté = chop and heat in a pan with a little oil) just before guests arrive, even if you are not serving onions. Your guests will assume you've been cooking all day. Related: Place any store-bought prepared food in your own dishes, and throw away the packaging before guests arrive. I'm not advocating deception—this is more of an effort in setting a homemade ambiance, right? (One friend of mine likes to mess up the frosting on store-bought dessert so it looks homemade.)

> *"Go thy way, eat thy bread with joy, and drink thy wine with a merry heart."*
>
> —*Ecclesiastes 9:7a*

Food should be fun. Is there a way you think you can make the project of feeding yourself fun?

_____

_____

_____

_____

_____

_____

_____

_____

_____

_____

_____

_____

_____

_____

_____

_____

_____

_____

_____

SMART Goal Setting!

SMART goal-setting brings structure to setting goals. SMART is an acronym for Specific, Measurable, Achievable, Relevant, and Timely.

Are you yawning yet? Me too, but this is good stuff. Pinky swear.

This approach to goal-setting is a great format to help write out and visualize your goals.

Let's break this down a little more:

> **Specific:** Who, what, where, when, why?
>
> **Measurable:** How much/how many?
>
> **Achievable:** Describe a result. Do you have the resources?
>
> **Relevant/Realistic:** Relevant to the degree/career path/dream/goal?
>
> **Timely:** When?

How does this apply to you and your goals? Identify a short-term goal below, like "cook a chicken breast." If you are vegan or vegetarian, maybe it's "cook a spaghetti squash." Use the SMART method to break down the steps below:

S _____

M _____

A _____

R _____

T _____

The Benefits of Routine

Are there benefits to routine? Like, really?

"Successful people aren't born that way. They become successful by establishing the habit of doing things unsuccessful people don't like to do."

–William Makepeace Thackeray

How Do Routines Impact Your Overall Quality of Life?

Ahhhh, routine. Routine is like a shelter from the chaos of life. Routine offers predictability; it can aid in helping break bad habits, establish new habits, and help us be more efficient. Hubba hubba . . . efficiency!

How Do Routines Impact Productivity?

"It is well to be up before daybreak, for such habits contribute to health, wealth, and wisdom."

–Aristotle

If Aristotle said it, then you know it must be worth adding to the list of things worth considering. (You have one of those lists, right? "Things Worth Considering." Just me? I digress.)

Routine helps lessen the thought and energy one must pour into a task, which saves thought and energy for tasks that *really* need resources. Routines help create a little "life autopilot" for us. How cool! In short, routines can help create *less* work. And less work is dope.

"My voice shalt thou hear in the morning, O LORD; in the morning will I direct my prayer unto thee, and will look up."

—Psalms 5:3

This verse suggests it might be advisable to rise and shine and hang out with God on a regular basis (nudge nudge), but what other routines might benefit you and your life? Can you think of any other routines (little autopilots) you can weave in to help remove a few extra layers of effort in your full life?

_____

_____

_____

_____

_____

_____

_____

_____

_____

_____

_____

_____

_____

_____

_____

Time Management and Priorities

> *"He that rises late must trot all day."*
>
> *—Benjamin Franklin*

I am a morning person, so my words favor sunrise over sunset. But I do love me a good sunset. . . .

What Can You Do on Sunday to Prepare for the Week?

- Update that planner/calendar

- Meal plan and prep (By "prep," I mean shopping, chopping, cooking, and divvying up prepped lunches and dinners into adorable, organized reusable containers.)

- Laundry

- Go to church (Start the week off strong; set the tone.)

- Call someone you love (mom?) whom you know you should call, but procrastinate. Eliminate the burden of guilt for the coming week.

- Note! "Sunday" doesn't *have* to be literally Sunday. Choose a calendar day or window of time when you can give yourself the gift of preparation.

You Can Do Anything, but You Can't Do Everything

Say it: "I can do *anything*, but I can't do *everything*."
Now write it.

_____

_____

In this building season of life, you get to make all kinds of choices: choices that will lead you down one path, which will lead to another, and another, and then one day you'll look up and wonder where you are and how you got there.

Zoinks!

Every decision points you in a direction. Period.

In what direction are your decisions leading you? A decision to eat that whole bag of Doritos may lead down a path of gastro-intestinal distress. It's remarkably easy to get distracted by the shine and sparkle of really good things (Oooh shiny!). Friends are good things! Concerts are good things! Spontaneity! Game nights! New cars! Pans of brownies! But try not to let these things distract you until your desired life path is shouting, "Hey, buddy, come back! I'm over here!" Write a prayer as you consider your path and this verse from Psalms 119:105: **"Thy word is a lamp unto my feet, and a light unto my path."**

_____

_____

_____

_____

_____

_____

_____

_____

_____

_____

How urgent is it?

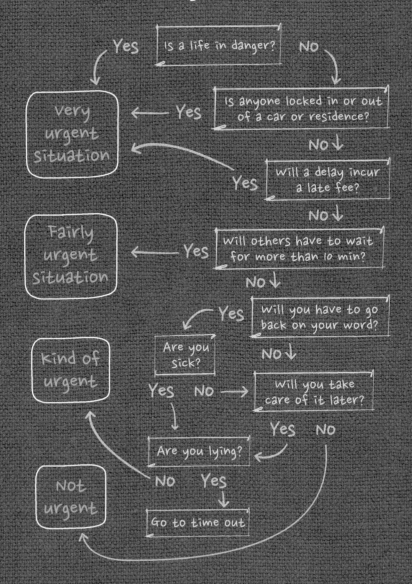

Yes ← Is a life in danger? → NO

Is anyone locked in or out of a car or residence? ← Yes → Very urgent situation

Will a delay incur a late fee? — Yes → Very urgent situation

Will others have to wait for more than 10 min? ← Yes → Fairly urgent situation

Will you have to go back on your word? — Yes → Are you sick?

Are you sick? — Yes / No

Will you take care of it later? — Yes / No

Are you lying? ← No / Yes

Are you lying? — No → Kind of urgent

Are you lying? — Yes → Go to time out

Not urgent

Checklist for Basic Adulting Survival

Things Actual Adults Do

- ☐ File and pay taxes

- ☐ Fix stuff that breaks

- ☐ Change the oil (or make the appointment to do so)

- ☐ Make doctor appointments (including the dentist)

- ☐ Make actual phone calls

- ☐ Give up summer break

- ☐ Know when to go to bed

- ☐ Think before speaking

- ☐ Check bank account

- ☐ Use a calendar

- ☐ Open and pay bills

- ☐ Learn to say "no"

- ☐ Have fun. Enjoy the journey. This is just as important as the rest.

"And into whatsoever house ye enter, first say, Peace be to this house."

—Luke 10:5

Chapter Three

Being the Kind of Person People
Want to Be Around

On Guest Etiquette

A few ideas on being your best guest-self:

- Pick up after yourself

- Offer to help

- Chew with your mouth closed

- Don't use all the hot water

- Don't overstay your welcome

- Bring or leave a small hostess gift

- Extra credit: Send a thank-you email . . . extra *extra* credit if it's a handwritten note!

Benjamin Franklin once wrote, "Fish and visitors stink in three days." Proverbs 25:17 notes, "Withdraw thy foot from thy neighbour's house; lest he be weary of thee, and so hate thee." Ouch. *And true.*

Have you experienced the friend or neighbor who wore out their welcome? What did they do that drove you nuts? (They're never going to see this.) What are your own thoughts on guest-ing? What are other ways you can extend good-guest vibes to your hosts?

_____

_____

_____

_____

_____

On Host Etiquette

Hosting (hospitality!) is easy with friends. If hospitality only applied to hosting people we like, we could delete this section, but hospitality isn't all about hosting fun parties for friends.

In Matthew 25:40, Jesus said that whatever we do for the least of people, we do for him.

What are some ways to treat guests with extra love?

- Use the nice dishes (or spring for the extra nice paper plates)

- Set out some candles or flowers

- Some say the devil is in the details (more work, maybe?), but I think God is. God is basically the greatest host of all—adding loving details all around us in flowers and seasons. We can do that, too. Maybe it's folding the hand towels in the bathroom and making sure there's an extra roll of TP in the cabinet. Or making sure you have that special drink on hand that you know is your guest's favorite. Small details can reveal most loudly how much you care, and that, my friends . . . is nailing the whole "host with the most" angle like a boss.

- Get prep done before guests arrive so you can focus on the people over the hosting tasks. Channel more of Mary than Martha. Read up on the Martha versus Mary drama in Luke 10:38–42.

- Another example of great hospitality is *Jesus*. He provided food for the thousands, he washed his disciples' feet (would you *ever* wash your guests' feet?), and he consistently welcomed and entered space with the most despised and rejected.

"Use hospitality one to another without grudging. As every man hath received the gift, even so minister the same one to another, as good stewards of the manifold grace of God."

—*1 Peter 4:9–10.*

Write out the passage below in your own words. What are a few ways not listed in the examples on page 39 where you can uniquely extend "hospitality to one another without grudging"?

_____

_____

_____

_____

_____

_____

_____

_____

_____

_____

_____

_____

_____

_____

_____

_____

What your body language says about you:

To communicate warmth and openness—smile!

To express exhaustion or lack of confidence—slump those shoulders

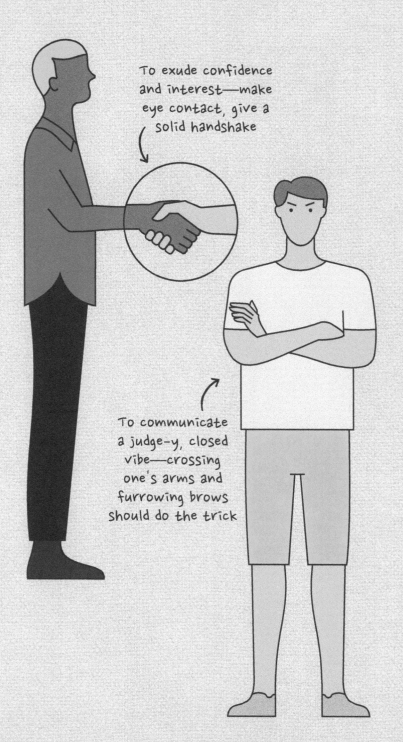

To exude confidence and interest—make eye contact, give a solid handshake

To communicate a judge-y, closed vibe—crossing one's arms and furrowing brows should do the trick

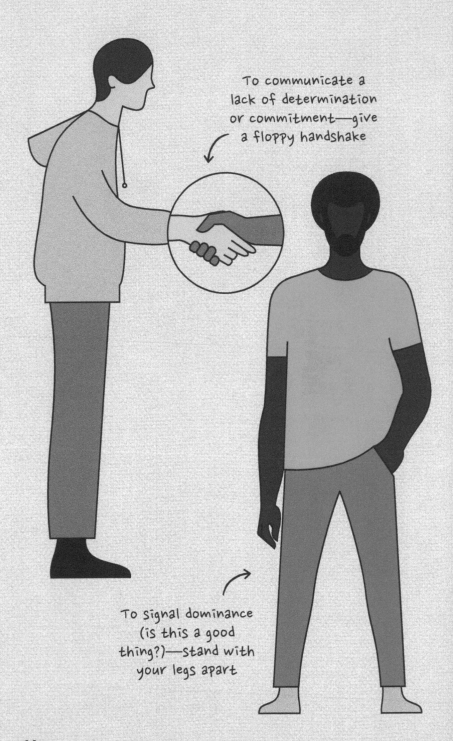

To show solid
judgment in the
face of boisterous
adversity—turn
and walk away

To communicate
interest—lean in

To send a message of
insecurity—pick at those
nails, avert your eyes

How to Change or Create a Habit

We all have them—bad habits. They are hard to break, perhaps even impossible. A quick Google search can tell you that the tried, true, and research-backed way is to replace bad habits with good ones. (Check out Charles Duhigg's *The Power of Habit* for a solid crash course.)

Breaking Bad . . . Habits

Deciding to not eat dessert every night may be a good way to help keep you from having to buy the next size up, for example. But if you pair that resolve with something else, like calling a friend or going on a walk or playing your guitar, your effort will likely be more effective.

The Bible offers some encouragement and a reminder when it comes to that pesky and persistent ol' battle of the mind in Romans 12:2: "And be not conformed to this world: but be ye transformed by the renewing of your mind, that ye may prove what is that good, and acceptable, and perfect, will of God."

Forming Good Habits

A Brief List on Forming Good Habits:

- Start small. Don't expect to go from couch potato to regular-exercising, kale-eating, vitamin-taking, ultimate to-do list tackling person in three days. Baby steps, baby.

- Read a book on the topic of habits (I suggest *Atomic Habits* by James Clear).

- Messing up *does not* equal failure. So you want to read your Bible every morning, but you slept in two days in a row? *Get back on it.* Don't let a failure erase your goal.

"I can do all things through
Christ which strengtheneth me."
—*Philippians 4:13*

Write Philippians 4:13 in a prayer below. Think about
a habit you would want to develop in your life and write
that out. Then put that verse on sticky notes. Post them
on your bathroom mirror, by your bed, at your desk, on
your computer or your coffee maker . . . put your goals
and good intent all up in your own face.

_____

_____

_____

_____

_____

_____

_____

_____

_____

_____

_____

_____

_____

_____

_____

_____

How to Hold an Adult Conversation

Get over yourself and get interested in others. IMHO, people who focus the convo on themselves are giving a monologue, not holding a conversation.

drops mic

picks mic back up because I have more to say

Ask questions. Listen. Don't rush to fill a silent gap. I know, I know. Silent gaps in conversation are awkward, but so is a foot in the mouth.

Proverbs 10:19 talks about people who talk too much. My paraphrase: More talk creates more opportunity to sin (be a jerk/misspeak). Wise folk know when to zip it.

Just try to be a good listener. You will have *plenty* of opportunity in life to use your words. I promise.

Know Your Audience

Know who you are talking to. We talk to our bosses differently than our BFF. We talk to other people's kids differently than we talk to a bartender. Is your post privacy on Facebook set to public or private?

The Bible gives some ideas on how we should or should not use our words. Proverbs 16:24 says, "Pleasant words are as a honeycomb, sweet to the soul, and health to the bones." And I just love the words in Proverbs 15:1, **"A soft answer turneth away wrath."**

Have you ever lost your voice? Did you notice that everyone you engaged with during those days of whispers also lowered their voice? Proverbs 15:1 isn't saying we should become whisperers. But think about a time someone responded to you in a gentler way than expected. What happened? Did it change your reaction?

It's important (even imperative) to be able to speak up and stand up for what is right.

And it's just as important to be able to read a room or situation. Write your thoughts on the struggles and benefits around speaking up versus holding your tongue. How does that work in real-life situations versus online conversations? Would you speak with your mouth the same words you type on a comment on YouTube or on a friend's post on Instagram?

_____

_____

_____

_____

_____

_____

_____

_____

_____

_____

_____

_____

_____

_____

_____

_____

Personal Mission Statement

Personal full-life-livin' mission statement time. Fill in the spaces below to create your own personal mission statement. Some questions to think about beforehand:

- Who are you, like really?

- What is unique about you?

- What do you want to accomplish?

- Why?

- How will you accomplish it?

- What is the main impact you want to make?

- Why is it important?

- What is your favorite verse?

I am _____ (your name).
As a _____ (career, dream, role) my mission is
to _____
(long-term goal, dream, hope). _____ ,
_____ , and _____
(character traits, core values) are important to me. These serve
as filters as I make decisions that affect the direction of my life,
my legacy. I want to make a positive impact because _____
_____
_____.

My life verse is, _____
_____
_____
_____

"A fool hath no delight in understanding, but that his heart may discover itself."

—Proverbs 18:2, a.k.a.: fools just keep runnin' their mouths.

Chapter Four

Adulting with Emotional Intelligence

Emotional IQ vs. Intellectual IQ

Academic intelligence is easy to assess and assign concrete value to. College entrance exams, anyone? What about emotional intelligence (EQ)? What about relatability, compassion, and knowing when to zip it versus when to speak up? Or how about just an ability to "read the room"?

Oh, and then there's social media. Social media has done a real number on us, particularly when it comes to our online EQ.

Apply Emotional Intelligence in Life and Work

In an article in the *Harvard Business Review*, researcher Claudio Fernández-Aráoz reveals research (everybody loves it when a book references "research") that emotional IQ is more important than intellectual IQ. If you struggle with your emotional IQ (and even if you think you don't), what are a few things to work on to help boost that EQ?

- **Self-awareness**—Pay attention to your emotions and how those emotions affect your mood, attitude, and decision-making. [Insert silent moment of reflection here.] Times of quiet prayer or meditation are great ways to peel away layers of distraction, like a stressed-out but mindful onion, as you seek to discover your core heart and motivation.

- **Empathy**—Simply put, love others. 1 John 4:7 says, "Beloved, let us love one another: for love is of God; and every one that loveth is born of God, and knoweth God." It doesn't matter if you understand or "get it" when another human is struggling or hurting, but in your effort to lead with love, you tap into empathy.

- **Self-management**—A.k.a. self-control, boo. In Proverbs 14:29 it says, "He that is slow to wrath is of great understanding: but he that is hasty of spirit exalteth folly." My personal synopsis is: *Respond* instead of *react*. A modern method might be the ol' "count backward from ten" approach, and take a moment to process and chill the heck out.

"Let nothing be done through strife or vainglory; but in lowliness of mind let each esteem others better than themselves."

—*Philippians 2:3*

Considering oneself second to another is not our knee-jerk reaction. In the space below, answer the following: Has there been a time in your life where someone has considered you above themselves? How did it make you feel?

_____

_____

_____

_____

_____

_____

_____

_____

_____

_____

_____

_____

_____

_____

_____

_____

Setting Boundaries

Emotional intelligence is a key ingredient in the complicated "recipe" of creating healthy boundaries. Setting boundaries often equals saying "no." Saying "no," whether or not you have a good EQ, is tough.

Establishing Boundaries

Boundaries are not selfish.

Write that: _____!

Folks (especially self-centered folks) tend to believe that "no" means you hate them.

That's on them. Not you.

The truth is, boundaries are an expression of love.

I realize that sounds like psychobabble, happy smack, but it's totes true.

Creating boundaries is a loving effort that honors both you *and* others. It's not just about saying "no," but about identifying and prioritizing the truly important.

How do you establish boundaries?

I am so glad you asked! There is a whole book on that (*Boundaries* by Drs. Cloud and Townsend, and I *highly* recommend it), but I'm going to distill it down to two super-important tasks:

- **Identify your goals.** How do you want to spend your life and time? What difference do you want to make in your life, community, world? When you have greater clarity on those things, it becomes clearer what will help you get there and what will be a distraction. I vote that you dig into God's word and talk to Him in the process. When you know your goals, and align them with God's word, decisions on yesses and those nos become clearer.

- **Get comfortable saying "no."** The expectations of others can make it hard to do the things that align with our goals. Having to say "no" or disappoint people can cause feelings of guilt (and even the s-word—*shame!*). *But*, if you have your goals and intent to help guide your deciding process, it is a bit easier to slough off the guilt others want to put on your back. Your purpose in life is not to please people; your purpose is to serve the Lord. He *wants* us to love others. In fact, He has *called* us to. Yet, isn't it funny that loving others does not equal doing or being what they think we should do or be?

*"Trust in the LORD with all thine heart;
and lean not unto thine own understanding.
In all thy ways acknowledge him,
and he shall direct thy paths."*

—Proverbs 3:5–6

*Take a few minutes to pray about your goals and
hopes for your life. Ask your heart, "Hey, heart,
what do you really want?" and write it in the
space below. Lay it all out to God. Explore what
your own unique path might be, and where you
believe God could be leading you.*

_____

_____

_____

_____

_____

_____

_____

_____

_____

_____

_____

_____

_____

_____

Divvy Up Your Social Pie

You love pie so much. You could eat an entire pie all on your own. However, just because you *can* doesn't mean you *should*. It'd taste really good, but later, "It seemed like a good idea at the time. . . ."

Your social life is a lot like pie. Too much of a good thing is entirely possible. Below are two social pies for you to enjoy. Divide one pie as your social life is currently divided and the other as you'd like it to be. Think friends, family, work, volunteering, clubs, CrossFit, that garage band you just started . . .

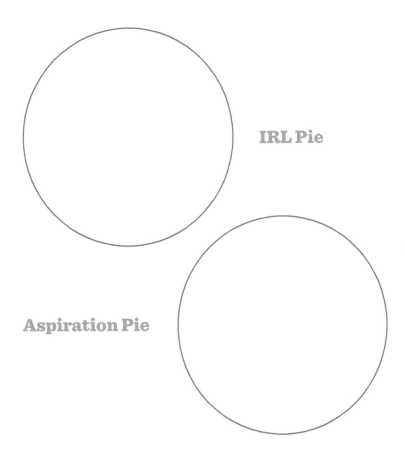

IRL Pie

Aspiration Pie

Prioritizing and Maintaining Important Relationships

Speaking of pie ... let's dish.

Healthy Relationships with Parents as Adult Children

Here's a hot one. You're grown and flown, but your folks didn't seem to get the memo.

Then there's the pressure of Exodus 20:12: "Honour thy father and thy mother: that thy days may be long upon the land which the Lord thy God giveth thee."

"But what about me and my adult independence?"

You always ask such great questions.

Let's Just Review That Boundary Thing One More Time

You still get to have and neeeed boundaries, including (perhaps especially) with your folks/family.

Creating boundaries is a loving effort that honors both you *and* others.

Creating boundaries is a loving effort that honors both you *and* others.

Now read it out loud, "Creating boundaries is a loving effort that honors both you *and* others."

Thank goodness you know yourself and are working on setting goals so you have your healthy boundaries in place, am I right?

Saying "no" may cause the fam feelings of hurt, and even anger (*gasp*), but bear in mind the words from Romans 12:18: "If it is possible, *as much as depends on you*, live peaceably with all men." You cannot control how others feel, but establishing healthy boundaries and pairing them with compassion (see also: emotional IQ) is loving.

Add a big dose of patience, too.

Speaking of patience—bookmark (or tattoo on your arm) Ephesians 4:2: "Be completely humble and gentle; be patient, bearing with one another in love."

Use the space below to write that verse out using fun pens or colored pencils. Have fun with creativity as you think about how boundaries and family relationships intersect with your own life.

_____

_____

_____

_____

_____

_____

_____

_____

_____

_____

_____

_____

_____

_____

_____

Get Comfortable with Boundary Setting

As you begin to design and define your own adulthood, boundary practices will shape your own future family and adult relationships. This is where that goal setting and boundary setting do a little mash-up and you get to be your own life designer and design the life you love.

Boundary setting with family is hard stuff, but if a soft answer turns away wrath (Proverbs 15:1), then surely God's word can offer some guidance (or at least encouragement).

Now that you've read a little more about boundaries, take a moment to reflect on your thoughts. How does it make you feel? It's okay to express your frustration, anger, hurt, and confusion. In fact, this could be a nice, safe place to release those negative thoughts and make space for some of that patience and gentleness . . . because you're gonna need it.

Dating and Finding a Partner/Intimacy

Where Do I Meet New People?

- Grocery store
- Church or religious community
- Volunteering
- Sport or activity club
- Coffee shop
- Museum
- Farmers' market
- Dog park
- Craft fair???
- Dance class with partner sharing
- The gym
- _____
- _____
- _____

Sound Advice on Looking for a Partner?

- ☐ Pray without ceasing. Like, seriously. (1 Thessalonians 5:17).
- ☐ Don't settle, be picky.
- ☐ Don't rush.

- ☐ When someone shows you who they are—believe them.

- ☐ Expect respect and know your worth.

- ☐ Pay attention to how they treat others (especially their own family).

- ☐ Want kids someday? Pick a partner who seems like they wouldn't suck as a parent.

- ☐ You are enough. A partner is not your completion, a partner is your complement.

- ☐ Seriously. You are fearfully and wonderfully made. You. Are. Enough (Psalms 139:14).

Navigating Faith and Finding a Partner

Faith, regardless of *what* faith you identify with, is pretty doggone important when it comes to the relationship sitch. Not liking the same TV shows as your significant other is one thing, but having a different faith can be a little trickier.

Faith plays a huge role in shaping our opinions, morals, parenting styles, career choices, political leanings . . . the list goes on. We all have qualities we look for in a potential partner, but making shared faith a priority can make it easier to know you're on the same page before you go down that mysterious tunnel of love. Let's face it, the whole lifetime commitment thing is hard, even with the most compatible of souls.

The absence of a shared faith can be challenging. But if you do choose that path, here are some things to consider before things get more serious:

- Will you raise your kids with religion? If so, which one?

- How will you handle family celebrations?

- Will both faiths be observed? Will one of the two of y'all convert?

- How about that wedding ceremony?

- Take a moment to think of other potential issues worth considering below:

  - _____

  - _____

  - _____

  - _____

  - _____

Being in a relationship means sharing the things that are important to you with Your Person™. If faith is a core value, you'll want to think about how it will fit into your partnership.

Can you just use the blank space below to draw a picture of a flower or rainbow or sunburst or a donut or SpongeBob SquarePants? I'm just feeling the need for a positive pause:

Didn't that feel good? Okay. Let's dig back in.

*"And this I pray, that your love
may abound yet more and more
in knowledge and in all judgment."*

—Philippians 1:9

*Seeking a partner requires sound judgment.
What feelings go through your mind as you dig
through this section? What are your own thoughts,
feelings, and/or struggles around faith, finding
a partner, and falling in love?*

_____

_____

_____

_____

_____

_____

_____

_____

_____

_____

_____

_____

_____

_____

_____

Handling Confrontation

How are you at handling confrontation?

Do you avoid it?

Do you attack it head on?

Somewhere in between?

What role does anger play?

Ephesians 4:26 says, "Be ye angry, and sin not: let not the sun go down upon your wrath."

The verse doesn't say, "Don't be angry." What it says is, "in your anger" don't sin.

Wait. *What*? Anger does not = sin?

It's true.

Anger isn't the issue. It's how we choose to handle the anger that matters. When you feel anger, it's time to have a chat with your bad (or mad) self and ask some questions:

- Is the situation a big or real deal?

- Am I just being sensitive and/or taking things personally?

- Does this issue even matter? Like really. Does it?

- If I "let it go," will the issue just fester, and become far worse in the end? FWIW, festering things are really gross.

- Am I prepared to speak the truth in love (Ephesians 4:15) and not in my own anger?

- Am I ready to be open to how I contributed to the issue?

- Can I give grace, mercy, compassion, and seek the mind-set of considering others better than me (Philippians 2:3)?

There are always exceptions, but considering average conflicts and issues, these questions are the first steps to get the problem-solving ball rolling.

When all is said and done, the situation may not resolve in the way you had hoped. You may not be offered an apology. You may have to agree to disagree (or worse). But you know what? *It is not our job to change someone's mind . . . or heart.* It's our job to love our neighbors (friends, family, guy who cut us off on the fast lane) and "*as much as lieth in you*, live peaceably with all men" (Romans 12:18). This applies to online commenting as well. Just in case there was any question on that.

"He that walketh with wise men shall be wise: but a companion of fools shall be destroyed."

—Proverbs 13:20

Chapter Five

Building Your Community

Growing a Diversified Support System

Where the heck to start?

- Where do you spend your time (work, school, grocery store, bus stop, library, church, gym, neighborhood)?

- Initiate contact and collaborate, create, build, change, and be changed!

- Where are you looking? At your phone? Heads up! Walk through your neighborhood sans earbuds. When in line at the store? Tuck that phone away! Pay attention to the life happening allllll around you, and say hello.

- _____

- _____

Staying Connected to Your Current Support Network

How hard can it be to stay connected? Surprisingly difficult. Social media gives us a false sense of connectedness. Just because we share select pictures of our lives on social, doesn't mean we are actually *social*.

What are ways to stay connected?

- Join a church and get involved. Your helping hands are invaluable, and it'll be hard to stay invisible.

- Set "standing dates." For example, I walk with a friend eeeearly every Tuesday and Thursday. Block out a time to meet with friends or a mentor on the reg. Or consider setting a "standing date" with a group—a craft sesh, running group, or pizza and beer night.

- If you are terrible at reaching out, set alarms on your calendar: "text sister," "email Hank," "call Angie." Remember Angie? She's that one gal you keep bumping into at the store. You *want* to hang out with her but you never follow through.

- Support someone who needs support. Nothing deepens connections more than becoming a helper.

- _____
  _____
  _____

- _____
  _____
  _____

Does it matter *who* you stay connected to? Signs point to yes.

"Be not deceived: evil communications corrupt good manners."

—*1 Corinthians 15:33*

In other words, when you hang out with people who are jerks, you become a jerk. When you hang out with awesome people, you can't help but channel awesome, too. Do you agree or disagree? List some character qualities you admire in others below. Think about your list as you spend time and energy building connections. What kind of people do you want to be part of your circle of influence (or, shall we say, "Personal Guidance Squad")?

Finding a Church Community

How might you determine what you need in a church to help your faith flourish?

- What are your priorities? Is worship super important to you? Does a diversity of programs float your boat? Does the church you are checking out share your passion for outreach, etc.?

- Consider having a sit-down with the pastor. Ask questions.

- Does the church have a statement of faith? If so, read it.

- Date the church. Don't feel like two visits = a lifetime commitment.

- Do you have to travel two hours to get there? Does having a church family far away make you feel more connected or disconnected?

Volunteer Life

Rhetorical question alert: Should you volunteer? Philippians 2:4 says, "Look not every man on his own things, but every man also on the things of others." In other words, duh. You definitely should.

Furthermore, serving others ends up serving the server far more than the served. Can you say that three times fast?

Related and obvious:

- Volunteerism doesn't have to be church- or faith-based.

- There are endless ways to serve—through organizations, schools, and don't forget the power of those individual random acts of kindness. No excuses!

I attended a meeting for yet another volunteer commitment just last night. As I drove away tired, cold, and particularly beat from the day, a few things dawned on me:

- Volunteering not only serves people in need, but it also blesses and helps the people we serve alongside.

- Volunteering with others establishes bonds with wonderful humans one may not have otherwise connected with. In my case, people I have volunteered beside have become some of my dearest friends.

When serving alongside others, you find good people with good hearts. *Those* are the people you want in your life and on your Personal Guidance Squad.

Where's your Bible (or Bible app)? Read Acts 20:35. It's that one passage about how it is better to give than receive. Can you think of a time where you found that to be true for you? Write an example below.

_____

_____

_____

_____

_____

The People Who Make Up Your Support System

Pencils up. Let's dig deeper. List five to ten character qualities you value in others.

_____

_____

_____

_____

Who are the people in your support system now? Who do you admire? Where did you meet them? Who knows how to talk you down and build you up?

_____

_____

_____

_____

Reflect on that list. Circle the names of those on the list above who have one or more of those character qualities that you admire. Is there a gap? If so, write that trait (or traits) below that don't have a person attached. Perhaps you can use the list to help fill in the gaps as you work to create your own Personal Guidance Squad.

_____

_____

_____

"This is the day which the LORD hath made; we will rejoice and be glad in it."

—Psalms 118:24

Chapter Six

Finding Joy

The Absolute and Utter Importance of Making Time for Self-Care

With such a big emphasis on serving, it is pretty easy to lose sight of the fact that we also need to care for ourselves. Even Jesus took time for that. Luke 5:16 says, "And he withdrew himself into the wilderness, and prayed."

Ugh, Self-Care Is *Everywhere*

Like, *everywhere*. Self-care is either very important or very on-trend. Or both.

You hear it all the time: "Put your own oxygen mask on first." You can't help others if you are passed out or dead.

What Actually Counts as Self-Care?

Self-care looks different for everyone. My self-care involves creative projects like macramé. Someone else might love cars, and their self-care involves working on engines. I have one friend who *loves* her hammock and another who *loves* hiking, but I can't tie macramé in a hammock or on a hike, so . . .

Do you make an effort to care for you? If so, what are a few ways *you* self-care? If you don't, what are some ways you can start?

Here's a recipe for a self-care reduction sauce:

- The self-care example Jesus set seemed to involve a lot of prayer [*nudge nudge*].

- Remember the chapter on boundaries? Review it.

- It's less about taking a bath, and more about preventing burnout. But baths are rad. Unless your tub is really dirty and it'll stress you out to clean it, then maybe just take a long, hot shower.

- Saying "no" to good things isn't bad. In fact, it can leave room for better things.

- Prioritize sleep.

- Drink water.

Why Caring for Yourself Is Another Way of Caring for Others

If your gas tank is on empty, you're not going anywhere. You can't help others if you can't move. Therefore, caring for yourself literally affects your ability to care for others. *drops mic*

"And let us not be weary in well doing: for in due season we shall reap, if we faint not."

—Galatians 6:9

*Hmmm . . . how does this verse support
the idea of self-care?*

_____

_____

_____

_____

_____

_____

_____

_____

_____

_____

_____

_____

_____

_____

_____

_____

_____

_____

Staying Connected to Your Passions

Speaking of self-care...

Are There Benefits to Doing the Things You *Love*?

Uh... *yeah. Duh!* Let's make a case for it!

- It provides a break, an escape, a point of refreshment. Yay, refreshments!

- It creates inspiration. Inspiration fuels us and pushes us and can have a lifelong ripple effect of awesome.

- It just makes us feel good, which helps keep us fueled.

- It's easy. We do hard things all the time. Easy isn't lazy—it can be an act of self-compassion as well.

- It can even help develop new skills, unless your self-care is binge-watching Zombie movies. But even then you're adding to your Zombiepocalypse survival skill set and that may be very helpful someday.

So, How Do You Stay Connected When "Busy" is Basically a Humblebrag?

Tip 1: Make time for it. Put it on your calendar, make it regular (weekly, first Saturday of the month, daily) and make no exceptions (remember that chapter on boundaries?).

Tip 2: Find someone who shares that passion with you. That "someone" can help keep you accountable, and you can be that for them, too.

"Commit thy works unto the Lord, and thy thoughts shall be established."

—*Proverbs 16:3*

Do you have any tips for maintaining connection? Is there anything you are doing now that seems to be working or not working?

_____

_____

_____

_____

_____

_____

_____

_____

_____

_____

_____

_____

_____

_____

_____

_____

_____

_____

The Importance of Sleep

Did you know sleep deprivation is used as a form of torture? *Sleep is awesome, you guys.* It is a *gift*. Sleep is the time when our bodies repair cells and tissue, store memories, and lack of it *stresses our bodies the heck out* which negatively affects the youthfulness of the skin, fat stores, and immune system, among other things. If I could turn back time (sung in my very best Cher impression) and I could change just one thing, I'd make sleep a top priority much sooner.

And moisturizer. Honestly, moisturize as much as possible.

TIRED HUMAN

- Forgetful

- Weight gain

- As dangerous a driver as a drunk

- Greater risk of stroke, heart attack, diabetes

- Angry

- Irritable

- Aged skin

- Depression

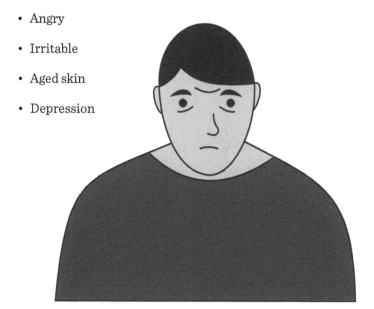

WELL-RESTED HUMAN

- Sharp and focused
- Happy, balanced
- Glowing skin
- Healthy heart and body
- Gets along better with others
- Mood booster
- Reduced stress
- Maintains weight
- Dialed-in immune system

"In the multitude of my thoughts within me thy comforts delight my soul."

—Psalms 94:19

This verse acknowledges the anxiety (and sleeplessness) our thoughts can bring, and the comfort God can give us in those times. Use the space below to pour out your thoughts. Release them to the comforting heart of God. Make space in your head for what He desires for you to carry instead.

_____

_____

_____

_____

_____

_____

_____

_____

_____

_____

_____

_____

_____

Enhancing Someone Else's Life

One of my greatest sources of personal joy comes from serving others. Research suggests altruism not only does good for others, but does good for ourselves, too.

"Serving others" doesn't mean you have to refill drinks, do laundry, and make beds. Acts of service are personal and incredibly varied, as are the people you bless through serving:

- Provide a meal (you don't have to make it—bring pizza!)

- Run an errand

- Send a thoughtful text (or letter)

- Sweep a porch

- Give a genuine compliment

- Volunteer *with* someone

- Pay it forward

- Pick up trash

- Put out the trash for the neighbor

- _____

- _____

- _____

- _____

- _____

*"For even the Son of man did not come
to be served, but to serve, and to give
His life a ransom for many."*

—Mark 10:45

*How have you served others in the past? What ways
have you seen others serve that have inspired or
made an impression on you?*

_____

_____

_____

_____

_____

_____

_____

_____

_____

_____

_____

_____

_____

_____

_____

"For which cause we faint not; but though our outward man perish, yet the inward man is renewed day by day."

—2 Corinthians 4:16

Chapter Seven

Tools for Tough Times

Recognizing and Getting Out of a Rut

How do you know when you are in a rut?

One time I took food to a friend because she just had a baby, and when I backed out of her driveway I backed right into a ditch.

Sometimes being in a rut is just that obvious. And sometimes it's hindsight, which isn't terribly helpful in the moment, but it is useful in moving forward and learning from past mistakes.

What are some indications that you might be in a bit of a rut?

- An overall feeling of apathy. You know, a general sense of "meh."

- Lack of oomph. Your usual zest is more like boiled cauliflower.

- A "just-get-by" mind-set.

Womp womp. That's no fun.

Asking for Help

There can be a fine line between being stuck in a rut and a more serious problem with depression. This is where asking for help is particularly wise.

In chapter 5, we explored the idea of building a community, and in chapter 6, we dug into finding joy. Flip back and look at the work you did there. What can you pull from those chapters to apply here? What steps in the process of self-care and staying connected can lift you out of a rut? Look to those in the community you are establishing (Personal Guidance Squad, anyone?) not only for advice, but for inspiration to inspire your way out of being stuck.

When Does a Rut Become Depression?

Depression is different from feeling stuck, yet being unable to get unstuck could be a contributing factor.

The following is a limited list from the Mayo Clinic of some signs that can indicate clinical depression: outbursts, irritability or frustration, loss of interest or pleasure in most or all normal activities, sleep disturbances (including insomnia or sleeping too much), tiredness and lack of energy, reduced or increased appetite, anxiety, agitation or restlessness, feelings of worthlessness or guilt, trouble concentrating or making decisions, and even physical manifestations.

If you suspect (even a little) that your rut has crossed into depression, call your doctor, reach out to a pastor, friend, or loved one, or call the National Suicide Prevention Lifeline at 1-800-273-TALK (1-800-273-8255).

We will always know struggle, but we also always have hope. God's word reminds us what to do and that He always has our back.

*"Even the youths shall faint and be weary, and the young men shall utterly fall: But they that wait upon the L*ORD *shall renew their strength; they shall mount up with wings as eagles; they shall run, and not be weary; and they shall walk, and not faint."*

—Isaiah 40:30–31

Do you believe the words in this verse? Are there other verses that have comforted you in dark times? Take a few minutes to write those verses here, or write out a prayer. Bear in mind the words from 1 John 5:15: "And if we know that he hear us, whatsoever we ask, we know that we have the petitions that we desired of him."

_____

_____

_____

_____

_____

_____

_____

_____

_____

_____

_____

Coping Gracefully with Tough Times

You guys. I am the actual *worst* at dealing gracefully with tough times. I take everything personally. In fact, I am so impatient I don't even have the patience to write about it.

Shame Won't Lead You Out

If I could go back and redo struggle in my life, I would go back with extra servings of grace for others *and* myself.

And I'd bury the shame and guilt in concrete. Like the mafia does to people in the movies. Shame has never provided a productive way out of tough times. Instead, a solid, honest look at the tough situation paired with a commitment to one's morals and convictions lead the way with love and compassion for others and oneself.

Talk It Out: Your Friends May Relate to More Than You're Aware Of

Why reinvent the wheel? Our friends have done some living. They likely have some resources and advice to offer. Think back to chapter 5 where you created that list of character traits you admire. It's those folks you can trust for help and support.

"Hear counsel, and receive instruction, that thou mayest be wise in thy latter end."

—*Proverbs 19:20*

How do you feel about going to your friends for support or advice? What might hold you back from reaching out?

_____

_____

_____

_____

_____

_____

_____

_____

_____

_____

_____

_____

_____

_____

_____

_____

_____

_____

_____

The Open Secret of an Abundant Mind-Set

"My brethren, count it all joy when ye fall into divers temptations; Knowing this, that the trying of your faith worketh patience."

—James 1:2–3

"Count it all joy . . ." Talk about mind-set! I'm not saying it's easy to find a positive when one gets a flat tire during rush-hour traffic, but if you aren't looking for that bright side, it will likely stay hidden.

Abundance vs. Scarcity

Instead of approaching life with a mind-set of lack (I don't have enough, I don't know enough, I have so little to contribute, etc.), approach life with the mind-set of what you DO have. This is not a practice in arrogance; it is recognizing your value and leaning into the beautiful, amazing, loved, imperfectly wonderful individual that you truly are. (God did not hold back when He got his creation on and made you with *tons* of worth.)

What value do you have to offer? Don't be shy.

_____

_____

_____

_____

_____

_____

Believing Everything You Need Is Available to You When It Seems Like It Isn't

I'm pretty cynical and TBH I really struggle with the whole "abundant mind-set" mentality. So if you struggle with buying in, *I get it*, friend. *I do.*

But I think we can move closer to the line if we can turn our head away from the negative and focus on the positive. If you are what you think ("For as he thinketh in his heart, so is he . . .," Proverbs 23:7a) then for crying out loud *put the brakes on negative thinking.*

It will be impossible to become or do or be or have something if you refuse to believe in the possibility, or worse—feel like you don't deserve goodness.

Shifting to an Abundant Mind-Set

You know how to make lists, right? In the space below, let's practice that skill. What *do* you have? What are you made of? What barriers have you overcome? What victories have been yours? Write these out so when thoughts of scarcity and negativity start steering you away from the path you should be on—you'll be ready!

*"But my God shall supply all your
need according to his riches
in glory by Christ Jesus."*

—*Philippians 4:19*

_____

_____

_____

_____

_____

_____

_____

_____

_____

_____

_____

_____

_____

_____

_____

_____

_____

_____

_____

Living Your Life to the Fullest

"Before I formed thee in the belly I knew thee . . ."

—*Jeremiah 1:5a*

God has known you from the beginning. We have not been created for a meh existence.

Amen?

In the spiritual, emotional, and tangible areas of your life, what are ways you can weave this idea of living life to the fullest in your own?

In Your Spiritual Life

- Read God's word

- Spend time in prayer and thankfulness

- Connect with a community/church

- _____

- _____

- _____

- _____

- _____

- _____

- _____

- _____

Emotional Life

- Dwell on the positive

- Ditch comparison thinking

- Set goals

- Keep a gratitude journal

- _____

- _____

- _____

- _____

- _____

Tangible Life

- Quit complaining already!

- Help others

- Be a starter, not a follower

- Assume the best in others. Until they give you a reason not to.

- _____

- _____

- _____

- _____

- _____

- _____

*"And whatsoever ye do in word or deed,
do all in the name of the Lord Jesus,
giving thanks to God and
the Father by him."*

—*Colossians 3:17*

_____

_____

_____

_____

_____

_____

_____

_____

_____

_____

_____

_____

_____

_____

_____

_____

_____

_____

Happiness Daily Checklist

Let's build those happiness muscles. Do these things enough and you might be surprised at how strong you have become. Note: Use this daily checklist as a guideline, not as law, and have fun with it. I mean, if you can't have fun with it, that kind of ruins the whole "happiness" purpose, so . . .

- ☐ Read the Bible and pray

- ☐ Drink water

- ☐ Deal with hard tasks first

- ☐ Smile—at others and even to yourself *

- ☐ Do something nice for someone else

- ☐ Exercise

- ☐ Name your blessings

- ☐ Choose positive thoughts, push away negative thinking

- ☐ Do something that contributes toward an important life goal

- ☐ Tidy up**

---

* Did you know smiling kicks off a chemical reaction in the brain? It releases hormones (like dopamine and serotonin), which give a little boost.

** A Princeton University study published in *Psychology Today* found clutter can make it harder to focus. A lack of focus is not a happy helper.

You know you are an adult when YOU notice something that needs to be done and YOU do it.
—Chris Gunnell
(actual adult)

"In all labour there is profit: but the talk of the lips tendeth only to penury."

—Proverbs 14:23

Chapter Eight

Getting the Job

Identifying a Field of Interest

So many choices! I was well into my junior year of college before I chose a major. Related: My career has nothing to do with what I went to college for. *Gasp!*

I asked in a Facebook post about choosing a career path and my friend Carrie Blankenship suggested, "Have a plan! [It] doesn't matter what that plan is—you are allowed to change your mind, but keep moving forward either in career or college or both. No standing still twirling your thumbs."

How does one decide?

Here are a few ideas to get that ball rolling:

- Make a list of what you love and just go ahead and pair your passions with potential occupations.

- Take a personality test . . . or two. Where does one find such tests for taking? Some community colleges offer them, therapists and counselors, and good ol' Google.

- Job shadow. If you think you are interested in something, connect with someone in the field. Most people love to help—firefighters, dental hygienists—ask around. In the words of Mister Rogers, "Look for the helpers. You will always find people who are helping."

- And, friend . . . what you choose now does *not* have to be your forever and always. Now is a board in the bridge to your becoming. Breathe, don't feel like this one decision is permanent.

- Your turn. List your own ideas:

  - _____
  - _____
  - _____
  - _____
  - _____

Think About What You Want to *Do*, Not What You Want to *Be*

Consider your talents and natural gifts. Consider the tasks you love to do versus the title you want to have. My friend Kristi suggests (rather wisely, I might add), "Try asking 'What problems do you want to help solve?' instead of 'What do you want to be?'"

Humility and Bravery at Work

What happens when you have a conflict at your job? Should you speak up or sit down?

In either situation, lead with love.

> *"Let all your things be done with charity [love]."*
> —*1 Corinthians 16:14*

If you face or witness adversity, oppression, or unfairness toward you or another in the workplace, choose your response through a filter and attitude of love. Responding with an attitude of love does not mean submission, but it can affect what words we choose and the attitude in which we deliver our words. Again, with Proverbs 15:1 where it says that a soft answer turns away wrath, yo.

- Defend the weak

- Stand up for what is right

- Have the wisdom to know which hill is worth dying on

- We don't have to be in agreement on everything

And this quote from Bob Goff, author of one of my favorite books, *Everybody, Always: Becoming Love in a World Full of Setbacks and Difficult People,* is 100 percent:

> *"Burning down others' opinions doesn't make us right. It makes us arsonists."*

*"And thou shalt do that which is right and good in the sight of the L*ORD*: that it may be well with thee..."*

—*Deuteronomy 6:18a*

Can you think of a time when you didn't stand up for someone or something? How can you prepare for next time?

_____

_____

_____

_____

_____

_____

_____

_____

_____

_____

_____

_____

_____

Entrepreneurship:
Starting a Business

I mean, who wants to work for The Man, when you can *be* The Man? Or y'know, THE HUMAN WITH POWER REGARDLESS OF GENDER.

But it's not all about Living the Dream. It's hard work, (been there) and a whole other level of responsibility.

Here are some things to keep in mind:

- Research! Is there a market for what you want to do or provide? What's the competition?

- Can you support yourself until the business starts earning? How? Be realistic about your time.

- Do you have a business plan? Do you know how to create one?

- Financing: Savings? Investors? Crowdfunding?

- Get a good bookkeeper, CPA, and/or attorney. They will provide services including

  - Business structure

  - Business registration

  - Licenses and permits

  - State and federal IDs

  - Trademarks

- Set up a separate bank account, and keep it separate

- Will you have employees?

- Where will you work? Home, office, coworking space?

If I could go back and do it all over, I would have would have hired a CPA out of the gate.

Interview Tips

- Research the company (and interviewers)

- Tighten up your social media (more on that later)

- Practice questions (recruit a friend and conduct a mock interview)

- Arrive early

- Arrive nicely dressed and clean

- Spit out the gum, sit up straight, and speak clearly

- Don't speak poorly about past bosses and coworkers

- Send a follow-up thank you email

"Let not your heart be troubled: ye believe in God, believe also in me."

—John 14:1

Patience and confidence can really take a beating during the interview process. List some of the amazing truths about yourself that no outcome can change.

_____

_____

_____

_____

_____

_____

_____

_____

_____

_____

_____

_____

_____

_____

_____

_____

_____

Salary Negotiation

Three things:

- Know your worth

- Just say "no" to self-deprecation

- Don't be an arrogant butt-face

When a Job Is Offered

Congratulations! Your hard work has paid off.

- Evaluate the offer

- Make a list of pros and cons

- You may need to consider making a counteroffer. Aaaaactually, companies frequently expect a counteroffer and have accounted for it in their offer.

- Remember it's okay to say "no."

- Be gracious regardless of the outcome. If you accept over the phone, it's good to accept in writing and confirm the terms. If you decline on the phone, also decline in writing and end on a positive, bridge-building note.

I am a *huge* believer in never ever (at least 99.8 percent of the time) burning bridges. A little bit of setting aside pride in order to walk away on good terms will likely come back around to serve you well. Networks are like the tide.

When You've Been Around Awhile

*"And as you wish that others would do to you,
do so to them."*

—Luke 6:31

Change can be hard, but monotony can present its own hardship. If you are ready for a change and want to leave, extend the courtesy of a heads-up to your employer. Don't leave them in a bind. Their good recommendation is priceless. Plus, it's just the right thing to do.

On the other hand, say you love where you are, and it has become easy and comfortable. Don't allow comfort to make you complacent. Always aim higher. "And whatsoever ye do in word or deed, do all in the name of the Lord Jesus, giving thanks to God and the Father by him" (Colossians 3:17).

When You're Offered a Promotion

Woot!

This is what you've been waiting for. Or is it? Weigh those pros and cons. Ask questions about the new role so you can decide if it fits with your goals and plans. In the next chapter, you get to create your own career mission statement. Consider new opportunities alongside your mission statement.

> *"The fear of the LORD is the beginning of knowledge: but fools despise wisdom and instruction."*
>
> —*Proverbs 1:7*

Do you think God has a plan or opinion on what job you take? What are some ways that you can honor God when you earn those sweet dollar bills?

_____

_____

_____

_____

_____

_____

_____

_____

_____

_____

_____

_____

_____

_____

_____

_____

_____

Should You Cover Your Social Media Footprints?

YES or NO

(circle one)

I have a good friend who is an HR professional, so I have it on good authority that social media profiles and online search results are, in fact, considered references.

Do you want to take that quiz again?

Let's just do a little homework. Get out your computer:

☐ Google thyself

☐ Change privacy settings on the socials (less is more)

☐ Profile and public pictures (any tacky grainy ones, questionable ones?)

☐ What do some of those old tweets say?

☐ Tend to that LinkedIn profile. Put a fresh coat of paint on that thing.

☐ Negative online persona? Any slander of a previous employer/next door neighbor/mom/stranger at the bank?

You know you're an
adult when you have a
favorite spatula.

—John Visser

(actual adult)

"And let the beauty of the Lord our God be upon us: and establish thou the work of our hands upon us; yea, the work of our hands establish thou it."

—Psalms 90:17

Chapter Nine

Keeping the Job

Emotional Intelligence in the Workplace

Take a moment and flip back to page 54 in chapter 4. We talked about the whole EQ thing a bunch more over there. Or I did. You read about it. I wrote about it. I digress.

Below, write the three things suggested to work on to help boost one's EQ.

- _____

- _____

- _____

Why Is EQ So Important in the Workplace?

Well, assuming you work with others at work (ahem), you most likely deal with issues related to collaboration, conflict, resolution of said conflict, and dealing with bosses. *Or* are you the boss now?

Either way, awareness of your own emotions, how emotion impacts your own behavior, and how it impacts others is mission critical in the workplace. Do you want to be able to pay the bills and buy alllll the concert tickets? *I know you do.*

Self-awareness, friend. Hang onto your good character . . . and that job.

A Quick List on Minding Your EQ at Work

- **Listen to others.** Active listening doesn't mean you must use ideas others pitch, but it helps others *feel* heard, which builds trust in a collaborative partnership and maybe earns you a few coveted recommendations on LinkedIn.

- **Be mindful of what stress and pressure brings out in you.** Rage? Tears? Snark? Consider counting to 10 . . . or 100 before reacting. If the struggle is *real* and you need to count to 10,000, say something like "I have some thoughts on this, but I am going to need to circle back." Then go to your cubicle, unroll the yoga mat, breathe in through the nose and out through the mouth, and watch a funny video on YouTube. Oh, and don't forget "A fool uttereth all his mind: but a wise man keepeth it in till afterwards" (Proverbs 29:11).

- **Don't step away to regroup and fail to step back in.** That's called avoidance and creates a whole new set of problems. Deal with issues ASAP. Short-term avoidance can help a little (a cool-down or wits-gathering period), but long-term avoidance in particular can be especially problematic.

- **Practice empathy.** If empathy is hard or not one of your natural "gifts," practice harder. Mindful and consistent integration of the points above are a great place to start, or Google "how to practice empathy." You'll find plenty of resources. I promise.

"And be ye kind one to another, tenderhearted, forgiving one another, even as God for Christ's sake hath forgiven you."

—*Ephesians 4:32*

Is there anyone that needs your forgiveness right now? How might forgiving them serve to benefit you today as well as the next time you feel wronged?

_____

_____

_____

_____

_____

_____

_____

_____

_____

_____

_____

_____

_____

_____

_____

_____

_____

_____

Tips for Clear, Professional Communication

- Effuse approachability

- Respond > react

- Kind eyes (angry eyes = negative body language)

- No gossip

- Ask for feedback
  [paper in hand reads "what do you think?"]

- "Assume others are doing the best they can"
  — Brené Brown

- Positive body language

- Ask questions: Seek clarity

Work Performance

"Let your light so shine before men, that they may see your good works, and glorify your Father which is in heaven."

—Matthew 5:16

In other words. your heavenly light shines when you work it, baby, and do your best.

What to Do When You're Struggling at Work

It takes perseverance and dedication to work out struggle. We have been conditioned to be able to solve most issues in one swipe left (or right). What should you do when you're struggling at work?

- Don't give up because it's not fast or easy

- Tap into your emotional IQ

- Make perseverance part of your work ethic. Count to 10.

There will always be exceptions, like a toxic boss or work environment. But here's the thing—even if you love what you do, it's *work*. Merriam-Webster's dictionary defines work this way: To perform or carry through a task requiring sustained effort or continuous repeated operations. Maybe nowadays workers don't have to carry everything uphill both ways because the office has an elevator (waves to grandpa from the thirty-eighth floor), but it's still work. Managing email, instant replies, and expectations may not wear out your actual muscles, but work is work is work.

Related: Struggle at work is not an exception; it's the rule.

Don't Join the Gripe Gang

"He that uttereth a slander, is a fool" (Proverbs 10:18). And for FWIW, "Let no corrupt communication proceed out of your mouth, but that which is good to the use of edifying, that it may minister grace unto the hearers" (Ephesians 4:29).

In short, don't gossip, . . . and don't be a Debbie Downer, either.

Really, this is no different than what we all learned in kindergarten. Play nice. Use kind words.

Yeah, it's work (womp womp), but you spend *a-stinking-lot* of time at work. It's where you make friends and build alliances for your life. *This* is your playground now, baby.

We considered people who deserve your forgiveness earlier in this chapter. Whose forgiveness do you need? What are some steps you could take to apologize and avoid allowing your emotions to cause harm to others?

_____

_____

_____

_____

_____

_____

_____

_____

_____

_____

Don't Be Afraid to Be a Beginner

"You've got to be a beginner before you can be anything else."

—*Anonymous*

History is *filled* with beginners: Johann Sebastian Bach, Martin Luther King, Jr., Mother Teresa, J. Lo, Julia Child, Jimmy Fallon, Will Smith, *Moses* . . . and if you want to be inspired by a story of a person who began and began and began and began, read a little about Abraham Lincoln.

And let's not forget about Thomas Edison. He had to start over 1,000 times to invent the light bulb.

What holds *you* back from beginning?

_____

_____

_____

_____

_____

_____

_____

_____

_____

_____

_____

_____

_____

"The things which are impossible with men are possible with God."

—*Luke 18:27*

Reflect for a moment on the encouragement in that verse. Do you believe that God's got you covered and can make all things possible? Do you want God to make something possible that isn't part of His ideal plan for you?

_____

_____

_____

_____

_____

_____

_____

_____

_____

_____

_____

_____

_____

_____

_____

Career Aspirations: Write Your Personal Career Mission Statement

Write out your personal career mission statement here. Refer to page 50 in chapter 3. See what you wrote for your personal mission statement for some inspiration. In this activity, include your skills, how they can benefit coworkers and workplace, and include your *why*. Why do they matter? When crafting this, consider both your short-term and long-term career goals.

Toilet paper costs REAL money. Be grateful for your parent's provision.
—Brian Norwood
(actual adult)

"Commit thy works unto the LORD, and thy thoughts shall be established."

—Proverbs 16:3

Chapter Ten

Career Development

Finding Mentorship

Riddle me this: What attributes do you admire in others?
Jot a few down here:

_____

_____

_____

_____

_____

A mentor is that one person you think is really smart and awesome and when you grow up you want to *be* them.

A mentor has struggled and worked through "the thick of it" and stands on the other side shouting out tips on how to make it through. Mentors help lead, encourage, and advise.

Looking at the list of attributes you listed above, can you think of a few people in your life that might be a good mentor for you? Write those names here:

_____

_____

_____

Perhaps there's a colleague you admire, a former college professor, a boss, or even your dad's retired business partner. A mentor could be someone not in your IRL circle—perhaps a podcaster or blogger you have admired for a long time with whom you are able to build a rapport or a connection on LinkedIn.

How Do You Know You're Being Mentored?

Mentorship is not born of "Hey, will you be my mentor?" Most mentor–mentee relationships are born of a natural progression as the relationship builds. The following is a totally made-up example, but I bet somewhere in the space-time continuum a very similar situation has played out over and over:

"I met Amy through a project we worked on together. She's was so professional, energetic, and creative! Eventually (we are both so busy), we connected over coffee where we talked business, and family life, too. I don't want to seem like a stalker so I'd never tell her this, but I can't help following her work. She sets such a high bar and is such an inspiration and mentor to me."

This Amy person may have no idea she is a mentor. But she is. A mentor relationship isn't a formalized contract. It's an organic relationship.

Thinking of mentorship through that lens, can you identify any possible mentors in your life?

"The way of a fool is right in his own eyes: but he that hearkeneth unto counsel is wise."

—*Proverbs 12:15*

In other words, don't be a headstrong fool. Wise people take advice. What do you think? What advice have you been given that deserves consideration?

_____

_____

_____

_____

_____

_____

_____

_____

_____

_____

_____

_____

_____

_____

_____

_____

Growing a Freelance Business

Freelancing can be legit *amazing*. It can also be the *worst*. What are some things a freelancer can do to tip the scales to favor the amazing side?

- Be a problem-solver for your clients. Focus on the *why*. You get to the root of solving the problem when you identify the *why* versus the *what*. Problem-solving builds referrals.

- Referrals are your most valuable resource. Knowing how to market your product is great, but nothing matches the power of a solid referral.

- Value yourself, but be willing to work for free in order to build your portfolio or gain experience. If you are just starting out, you may need to build your own street cred.

- Charge more than you're comfortable with. You can always come down. But if you quote low out of the gate, there goes that wiggle room.

- Connect with people in the same or similar industry and be a question-asker. What are similar problems you are both solving? See also: mentorship.

- Apply that emotional intelligence.

- Create a persona of your ideal customer or client. Give them a name and a personality. As you develop your strategies, you will have an idea of whose problems those strategies will help solve.

(Continued)

- Establish a process—your way of solving problems—and communicate that. A good doctor gives a tremendous amount of relief just by saying, "This is how we're going to do it."

- Focus on what's in your wheelhouse, and then hire others to do the things that keep you from doing what you are best at.

- Establish a place where you can work and that gives the ability to take calls in a professional environment.

Growing Your Career

In order to grow in your career, you need to show how you add value to the team. One surefire way to create value is developing a reputation as a problem-solver.

Oh, and commitment to lifelong learning! Look for certifications in your field, seek continuing education opportunities, read articles, attend industry conferences, _____ , and _____.

Inside Your Current Company

There are countless ways to work toward career growth within your current company. Here are a handful to get you started:

- Be the solver of problems for the people around you.

- Be honest, genuine, and transparent.

- Make your boss and his/her boss look *awesome*.

- Do what you say you are going to do, and if something changes, communicate it ahead of time. *Show up*.

- Don't discount lateral moves that give you even more potential. Look and interview for jobs inside your own company.

Networking in the Outside World

Networking is kind of fun. But don't let that distract you from the fact that *you are laser focused*. Some networking-type things to consider:

- Everyone you meet is a potential future job.

- Immediately follow up (email, LinkedIn) with anyone you meet (parties, conference, a random meeting at a coffee shop, church) whom you think could be a meaningful connection. Do it while the connection is fresh.

- Attend industry conferences, after parties, and company functions. Be social. But also be mindful of the bar.

- LinkedIn. Give recommendations.

- Build, build, build those bridges. You literally cannot predict how far a bridge will take you, or when it will come back over your river of work.

*"Who then is a faithful and wise servant,
whom his lord hath made ruler over his
household, to give them meat in due season?
Blessed is that servant, whom his lord
when he cometh shall find so doing. Verily
I say unto you, That he shall make
him ruler over all his goods."*

—Matthew 24:45–47

*The passage is basically this: Your boss gives you
responsibility and leaves the office. While the boss is
away, you work hard (instead of playing Minecraft
on your phone). The boss returns and, because
you rocked it, you get a raise and a promotion.
Is this just a Bible story or do you think this
scenario is likely to mimic real life?*

_____

_____

_____

_____

_____

_____

_____

_____

_____

_____

Being a Good Leader

What makes a good leader? I have no doubt you already know. You have met lots of leaders in your life:

- They make the best opportunities for their team. They know and care about the dreams and passions of each individual.

- They actively look for ways to connect others with opportunities to achieve their goals.

- Good leaders are not necessarily out front.

- They remember the personal things. Yes, it's a job, but showing empathy or interest shows that emotional intelligence we've been talking about.

- A good leader enables others to do their job but doesn't do their job for them.

- Serve. It's the opposite of the power-leader model, but these leaders are more effective and are leading through example.

> *"But whosoever will be great among you, let him be your minister."*
>
> —*Matthew 20:26*

In other words, if you want to be great, be a servant. This even goes for bosses. Do you agree? Why or why not?

_____

_____

_____

_____

_____

_____

_____

_____

_____

_____

_____

_____

_____

_____

_____

_____

_____

SMART Goal-Setting at Work

In chapter 2 we broke down SMART goal-setting for life in general. Let's review what the acronym stands for and what type of questions you can ask yourself as you approach work goals using this system:

Specific: Who, what, where, when, why?

_____

Measurable: How much/how many?

_____

Achievable: Describe a result. Do you have the resources?

_____

Relevant/Realistic: Relevant to the degree/career path/ dream/goal?

_____

Timely: When?

_____

Based on the information above, can you come up with any specific questions using SMART goal-setting that will help you set goals today?

_____

_____

_____

_____

"Let your conversation be without covetousness; and be content with such things as ye have: for he hath said, I will never leave thee, nor forsake thee."

—Hebrews 13:5

Chapter Eleven

Get Smart About Money

Money Management

"Manage your money, or it will manage you."

—Me

Budgeting

Go ahead. Lament. Get it out.

_____

_____

_____

_____

_____

_____

_____

_____

_____

_____

You good? OK.

Here's the thing: Creating a budget isn't all that difficult. It's the *sticking to a budget* that is a legit drag.

Sticking to a budget often means saying no to fun stuff, cool stuff, and convenient stuff. Sticking to a budget may make you feel like a stick-in-the-mud, or like you are turning into your mom.

Welcome to adulting. One reason childhood was so rad was because the adults were the ones who had to make the call on sticking to a budget.

Living Within Your Means

What does "living with your means" mean?

_____

_____

_____

_____

_____

The simple answer:

If you have $1,000 for the week, you have $1,000 for the week. That's living within your means.

Real-life example:

Living within one's means = starting with the essentials: Pay rent and bills, stock the fridge, and fill the gas tank. Take care of debts including but not limited to Venmo-ing your bestie for covering that T-shirt you got at Supreme and dinner last week because you forgot your wallet.

Furthermore, Starbucks is not an essential. Nor is that T-shirt from Supreme.

If you end up needing to borrow money for rent from the parentals, the roomie, or the local cash-and-loan . . . you are not living within your means.

Have you ever tried walking down a dirt hill on a rainy day? That's a slippery slope, and what it's like to live beyond your means.

"Get wisdom, get understanding: forget it not; neither decline from the words of my mouth. Forsake her not, and she shall preserve thee: love her, and she shall keep thee. Wisdom is the principal thing; therefore get wisdom: and with all thy getting get understanding."

—*Proverbs 4:5–7*

This passage is all about wisdom—using it, obtaining it, not forgetting it, and the blessing of it. It is not about using, obtaining, or the blessing of money. How does this verse apply to you as it relates to money? In what ways can wisdom impact how you manage your money?

_____

_____

_____

_____

_____

_____

_____

_____

_____

_____

_____

Why You Need Credit

Credit can be super useful, but it can also be really dangerous. I vote for proceeding with some caution.

Establishing credit is important. For example, to obtain a mortgage loan, or other large loan, you need to have a history of credit—preferably a *good* one. To establish good credit history, you need to establish credit.

To establish good credit history:

- Use credit.

- Pay it on time.

- Pay it off.

- Don't take out too much credit.

To tank your credit score:

- Acquire lots and lots of credit cards.

- Maintain balances on those lots and lots of cards.

- Make a late payment every now and then.

- Max everything out.

Pro tip 1: Having many credit inquiries (applying for the TJ Maxx card, the Target card, the American Eagle card, the Apple card . . .) can count against your credit score. The banks will be like, "What empire are they planning to fund with all that borrowed money?" Sure, you'll get 10 percent off at Old Navy on your *entire* purchase when you open that card, but think—how many of those cards/credit inquiries have you acquired? Too many will lower your credit score.

What is a credit score? It's basically the grade you get on life's big test on how you use your credit. Your score qualifies you (or disqualifies you) for loans, and even some landlords check credit scores as part of their vetting process. Visit www .experian.com/blogs/ask-experian/credit-education/score -basics/what-is-a-good-credit-score/ to learn what scores are good, bad, and in between.

Pro tip 2: Monitor your credit history and score. You can get a free copy of your credit report every year. You are permitted by law to access this information by calling Annual Credit Report at 1-877-322-8228 or visiting AnnualCreditReport.com. You will receive a report from each of the three credit reporting companies that collect your information: TransUnion, Equifax, and Experian.

Do you have any credit cards or loans right now? Make a list of them below, and for added homework, find out and write down what percentage interest you are paying on each loan or card.

_____

_____

_____

_____

_____

_____

_____

_____

_____

_____

How does that list look? Are there many? Are you paying on time? Do you feel you are living within your means? Do you know your credit score?

You may be able to list off the credit cards and loans you are currently paying on in your head, but sometimes seeing things laid out on paper makes things really real. Break out your pencil, and maybe a calculator, and let's see how many debt dollars fly out of your bank account each month:

Card/Loan Name	Card/Loan Balance	Card/Loan Monthly Payment
_____	_____	_____
_____	_____	_____
_____	_____	_____
_____	_____	_____
_____	_____	_____
_____	_____	_____
	Total debt:	**Total Monthly Payments:**
	_____	_____

What to Be Aware Of

If you must open a credit card, open one with rewards, so you get a little something extra (like airline miles or cash back). When you use said card, go straight home (or open the app) and pay off your charges immediately. Some people are really good about paying off the credit card every month.

I always thought I would be.

Reality check: *I am the* actual worst *at paying off ye olde credit card every month.*

Pro tip: Know thyself. How are you about paying off debt? Be honest! If you have yet to use credit, use the space to write a commitment statement regarding the wisdom of working to live within your means.

_____

_____

_____

_____

_____

_____

_____

_____

_____

_____

_____

_____

The problem with using a credit card is that it adds up. *You blink and you have suddenly spent past your budget and now you are living beyond your means.*

It takes discipline. Period. There's no fluffy, feel-good way around this. Manage thy credit or thy credit companies will manage thee.

"For wisdom is a defence, and money is a defence: but the excellency of knowledge is, that wisdom giveth life to them that have it."

—*Ecclesiastes 7:12*

In other words, both wisdom and money are shelters, but wisdom is better than cold, hard cash. Why would the Bible feel it is so important to highlight this?

_____

_____

_____

_____

_____

_____

_____

_____

_____

_____

_____

_____

_____

_____

Balanced Budget Pie

The pie you're about to bake will impact your financial health for the rest of your life, so choose your ingredients carefully! You can use the adult-vetted recommendations below as a guide to slice up your dollars. Don't bite off more than you can chew!

- Tithing/giving: 10%
- Saving: 5–10%
- Housing costs: 25–28%*
- Food: 5–15%
- Utilities: 5–10%
- Transportation: 10–15%
- Insurance: 5–10%
- Recreation: 5–10%
- Personal spending: 5–10%
- Miscellaneous: 5–10%

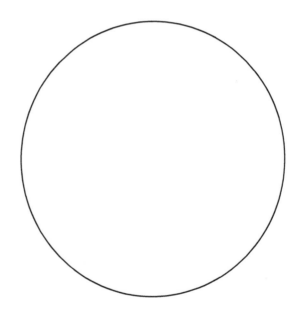

---

* Housing costs can vary a lot depending upon where you live. If your home is in a city, for example, your housing costs might be a higher percentage of your budget pie.

Value Yourself

What are your thoughts on the phrase "Value yourself"? Is it hard for you to do? Why or why not? Do you feel it's important? Why or why not?

_____

_____

_____

_____

_____

_____

_____

_____

_____

_____

_____

_____

_____

_____

_____

_____

_____

"I will praise thee; for I am fearfully and wonderfully made."

—*Psalms 139:14a*

You are valuable. Period.

"Value yourself" does not mean be an arrogant jerk. Valuing yourself is receiving the compliment. It is recognizing you (your time, your heart, your gifts, your very being!) are a vital piece of this crazy puzzle of life. Valuing yourself means accepting that only the raddest things come from God's hands, including you.

How does this play out in real life?

- It's okay to turn down "opportunities." Ask yourself, "Is this really an opportunity or am I just hungry/desperate/insecure?"

- Remember boundary setting from chapter 4? Setting boundaries is the pro-legit way to exercise the practice of valuing you.

- Comparison. Don't. "Don't compare your beginnings to someone else's middle."—Tim Hiller, *Strive: Life Is Short, Pursue What Matters*

- Get out of your own head. Memorize this verse from 2 Timothy 1:7: "For God hath not given us the spirit of fear; but of power, and of love, and of a sound mind."

"What lies behind you and what lies in front of you pales in comparison to what lies inside you."

—*Ralph Waldo Emerson*

Acknowledge, name, and claim your awesome value right here! Be specific! Compliment yourself! If it's just too hard, turn this space into a prayer of thanksgiving to God, but be specific, OK?

_____

_____

_____

_____

_____

_____

_____

_____

_____

_____

_____

_____

_____

_____

_____

_____

"He that hath
no rule over his
own spirit is like
a city that is
broken down, and
without walls."

–Proverbs 25:28

Chapter Twelve

Don't Spend It All in One Place

Master Your Willpower

Can you do it? Is it possible to master your willpower? Why or why not?

_____

_____

_____

_____

_____

The best way to master willpower is to create an environment for success and eliminate tempters.

- Want to eat less junk food? Instead of buying a box of donuts and willpower-ing yourself to eat just one, just buy one donut.

- Want to spend less? Instead of resisting online purchasing by deleting store emails one by one, unsubscribe forever.

- And tuck this guy in your back pocket/heart for added measure: "Trust in the Lord with all thine heart; and lean not unto thine own understanding. In all thy ways acknowledge him, and he shall direct thy paths" (Proverbs 3:5–6).

You don't have to pass a test to be successful!

Create an environment that ensures a greater chance of success. For example, if you stay up too late watching TV in bed, remove the TV from your room. Voila. More sleep.

Willpower Fatigue

Some call it "willpower fatigue"; others call it "decision fatigue."

In either case, defeating this fatigue comes down to habits, yo. Habits are handy systems (or little automations) we create that help remove the decision process. It creates an additional level of separation from temptation.

By creating habits, we take the decision (temptation) out of the action. It's like becoming part robot. So long, decision fatigue!

Author James Clear, in *Atomic Habits,* writes,

> *"You do not rise to the level of your goals. You fall to the level of your systems."*

In other words, setting goals is fantastic, but reaching them depends on the path of small actions leading to your goals. Habits and systems work to automate our behavior so our willpower isn't the only path to change.

When it comes to willpower fatigue and spending, can you think of where willpower fatigue affects your spending decisions?

_____

_____

_____

_____

_____

_____

_____

_____

Mental Muscle Memory

A.k.a. "habits," those acquired behavior patterns that, over time, can become almost involuntary. But much like superpowers, they can be used for both good and evil.

Make a list of your own habits. In the left column, identify the habits that may hinder you, and in the right column, identify habits that help you.

Hindering Habits   **Helpful Habits**

_____   _____

_____   _____

_____   _____

_____   _____

_____   _____

_____   _____

_____   _____

_____   _____

_____   _____

_____   _____

_____   _____

_____   _____

_____   _____

_____   _____

"Watch and pray, that ye enter not into temptation: the spirit indeed is willing, but the flesh is weak."

—*Matthew 26:41*

It's time to dig deep. Think about temptation. What habits can you work on developing to help empower you as you work toward your adulting life goals? Speaking of, have you identified your adulting life goals?

_____

_____

_____

_____

_____

_____

_____

_____

_____

_____

_____

_____

_____

_____

What Should Your House Payment Be?

As a general rule, a monthly rent or mortgage payment should not exceed 25 to 28 percent of your gross (before tax) monthly income.

If your monthly income is $2,000, multiply that by 0.25 for a grand total of $500. That's the max amount a mortgage should cost. Twenty-eight percent is the magic maximum number lenders consider.

Let's take a look at how much you can afford.

Take your gross monthly income multiplied by 25 percent (0.25) to get that handy little answer.

_____ × _____ = _____

That amount is the most your house payment should be. Dave Ramsey has a handy-dandy calculator at www.daveramsey.com/blog/how-much-house-can-i-afford or use the Zillow mortgage calculator if you want to play with the numbers a little bit.

IMPORTANT NOTE: Consider keeping homeowner's insurance and property taxes with mortgage payments in an escrow account (an account held for money your lender uses to pay those property taxes and homeowner's insurance bills). Homeowner's insurance and property taxes add up and increase that monthly payment by hundreds. Combining them in one payment (this is where that escrow account comes in) might increase the monthly payment, but will you have a few thousand saved up to pay off a property tax account each year? It's something to think about.

Should You Rent or Own?

To rent or to own, that is the question.

- **Money and getting settled:**

  - Renting: First month's rent, last month's rent, security deposit, setup costs (electricity, garbage, water, etc.), renters insurance

  - Owning: Down payment (usually 20 percent of the cost of home), setup costs (electricity, garbage, water, etc.)

- **Maintenance:**

  - Renting: Most maintenance falls on the landlord (if the pipes burst or general repairs not related to breaking things due to renter's fun and games and general clumsiness).

  - Owning: You fix the fridge, you replace the faucet, you replace the roof, you do eeeverything (or pay someone).

- **Negotiation:**

  - Renting: It doesn't hurt to ask. The ask doesn't have to be for a lower rent payment (but that sure is handy). You can negotiate a waived deposit or for covered parking to be included.

  - Owning: You can purchase a home without a real estate agent, but it is not recommended. They know the market. A good agent will know the neighborhood and may even have inside info on the property. Some argue using a good agent has the potential to save you money.

Benefits of Renting

1. Less repair liability
2. Flexibility (limited lease length options)
3. Less cash up front
4. Amenities (a pool, a gym...)
5. You're not stuck with problem neighbors [*wink*]

Benefits of Owning

1. It's an investment
2. Interest write-off on taxes
3. More control of the property (you can remove wallpaper and create all the nail holes you want!)
4. Predictable house payment (versus crazy landlords who like to raise rent)
5. Appreciation. Sure you'll appreciate a place of your own, but this appreciation has to do with investment appreciation. Property typically increases in value, so it can be a great investment.

What Should Your Car Payment Be?

Great question. Here are some other questions:

- What's your income?

- How much debt do you have?

- How's that credit score?

According to Credit Karma, 15 percent of your net income is a good general number.

$_____ (net income) × 15 percent = _____ (car payment)

Pro tip: Don't forget about insurance and the cost of maintenance.

Buying a Car

Roll up your sleeves because adulting is about to get *really real.*
Let's make this a true-or-false quiz. Circle the correct answer.
When buying a car . . .

> **true** or **false** — Set a budget
>
> **true** or **false** — Make a list of features you require
> and want
>
> **true** or **false** — Walk in with prefinancing
> (financing secured)
>
> **true** or **false** — Research your vehicle options, keeping
> in mind ownership cost
>
> **true** or **false** — Shop around
>
> **true** or **false** — Test drive vehicles of interest
>
> **true** or **false** — Negotiate
>
> **true** or **false** — Don't be afraid to walk away

If you answered *false* to any of the questions, do not pass go,
and do not collect $200.

Be Prepared to Walk Away

Really, there's not much to add to that.

If dealing with a salesperson, they'll talk to their manager and
bring you an offer that exceeds all offers they have ever given
ever in all their years of operation. If dealing with a person from
a listing you found on Craigslist, meet up in a public place and
maybe bring your friend with the most muscles and tattoos.

Know stuff. Research is *king.* If the vehicle of interest is used,
insist you take the car for a few hours to have your mechanic
give it a once-over.

If the seller flatters you, sweet talks you, or employs tactics of fine manipulation, go back to your foundation. *Know what you can and cannot do.*

Be unswayable. Be prepared to call their bluff and walk away. They may call after you when your awesome, adulting seriousness is realized. And if they don't, it's OK. The possibility that you just walked away from the deal of a lifetime is . . . not probable.

> *"There hath no temptation taken you but such as is common to man: But God is faithful, who will not suffer you to be tempted above that ye are able; but will with the temptation also make a way to escape, that ye may be able to bear it."*
>
> —*1 Corinthians 10:13*

The part of the verse that says God will make a way to escape temptation—so cool, right? What are some ways you can prepare for that escape when you are sitting at the bargaining table?

_____

_____

_____

_____

_____

Negotiate Like a Car Salesman

Or, do you really *want* to negotiate like a car salesman? Sure, they might be known for getting the number they want, but they are also known for being not the most forthcoming when it comes to numbers. Knowing how to play their game will help you avoid getting taken for a ride.

Are you a good negotiator?

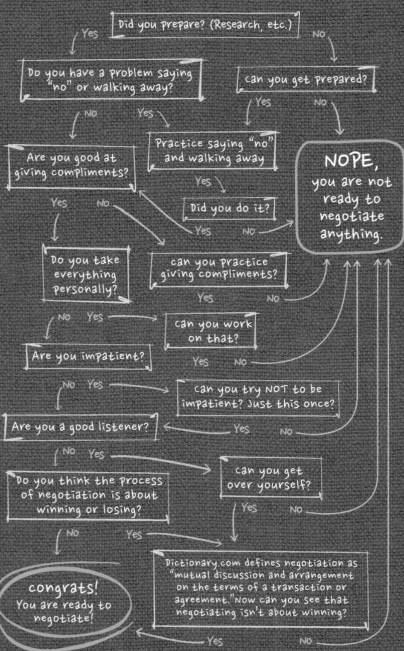

Did you prepare? (Research, etc.)

Yes → Do you have a problem saying "no" or walking away?

NO → Can you get prepared?
- Yes → Practice saying "no" and walking away
- NO → **NOPE, you are not ready to negotiate anything.**

Do you have a problem saying "no" or walking away?
- NO → Are you good at giving compliments?
- Yes → Practice saying "no" and walking away

Practice saying "no" and walking away
- Yes → Did you do it?
  - Yes →
  - NO → **NOPE, you are not ready to negotiate anything.**

Are you good at giving compliments?
- Yes → Do you take everything personally?
- NO → Can you practice giving compliments?

Can you practice giving compliments?
- Yes →
- NO → **NOPE, you are not ready to negotiate anything.**

Do you take everything personally?
- NO →
- Yes → Can you work on that?

Can you work on that?
- Yes →
- NO → **NOPE, you are not ready to negotiate anything.**

Are you impatient?
- NO →
- Yes → Can you try NOT to be impatient? Just this once?

Can you try NOT to be impatient? Just this once?
- Yes →
- NO → **NOPE, you are not ready to negotiate anything.**

Are you a good listener?
- NO → Can you get over yourself?
- Yes →

Can you get over yourself?
- Yes →
- NO → **NOPE, you are not ready to negotiate anything.**

Do you think the process of negotiation is about winning or losing?
- NO → **congrats! You are ready to negotiate!**
- Yes → Dictionary.com defines negotiation as "mutual discussion and arrangement on the terms of a transaction or agreement." Now can you see that negotiating isn't about winning?

Dictionary.com defines negotiation as "mutual discussion and arrangement on the terms of a transaction or agreement." Now can you see that negotiating isn't about winning?
- Yes → **congrats! You are ready to negotiate!**
- NO → **NOPE, you are not ready to negotiate anything.**

"Thou shalt truly tithe all the increase of thy seed, that the field bringeth forth year by year."

—Deuteronomy 14:22

Chapter Thirteen

What to Set Aside

Charity and Tithing

Anne Frank wrote, "No one has ever become poor by giving." And the good ol' Bible notes in Acts 20:35, "It is more blessed to give than to receive."

There's data to back that up. Research proves giving literally benefits the life of the giver. Not only are people who give happier, studies also show that givers tend to outearn nongivers.

I recently read *Give and Take* by Adam Grant and . . . wow. I am not telling you to go get that book, but I'm not telling you not to. I wish I'd had the influence of the thoughts on give and take shared in *Give and Take* when I was in the early part of shaping how I give. In chapter 12, we talked about valuing oneself. Pairing that concept with a healthy approach on giving (of self and resources) has the potential to create a powerful and life-changing impact.

We are all called to love one another. If we are loving others, giving will be an integral part of showing the love. There's a saying that "less is more," but when it comes to love, you have to admit, more is more.

*"Give, and it shall be given unto you;
good measure, pressed down, and
shaken together, and running over,
shall men give into your bosom.
For with the same measure that
ye mete withal it shall be measured
to you again."*

—Luke 6:38

*God's word and scientific research are both trying to tell
us that giving is where it's at. Are you in the practice
of tithing? What are other ways you can give, or ways
you already do (charity and offerings)?*

_____

_____

_____

_____

_____

_____

_____

_____

_____

_____

_____

_____

_____

_____

Saving and Investing Your Nest Egg (401(k)/IRA, etc.)

What on earth are those things?!

It's OK. I've got your back. Actually, Investopedia has your back:

A 401(k) is a tax-deferred retirement savings account offered by employers to their employees. Employees contribute money to their account and employers can choose to match a percentage of that contribution.

An individual retirement account (IRA) (traditional or Roth) is a tax-deferred retirement savings account established by an individual person. SEP and SIMPLE IRAs are offered by employers to their employees. They are similar to 401(k) accounts in many ways, but there are some differences.

One of my own biggest adulting regrets . . . *not prioritizing saving, you guys.*

There are lots of things that get harder to do with age. Here are a few:

- Gymnastics

- Picking up large, heavy objects

- Reading books without glasses

- Saving money

If you take nothing away from this book but one thing—take this one thing *please*:

Get in the habit of saving yo monies.

Life doesn't get cheaper. There will rarely be a better time than now to start saving. Don't discount the value of saving one dollar at a time. *Plus?* You have the benefit of time, so what you save has a long life of earning potential (yay interest).

For the love of yourself and the people who may have to empty your bedpan in seventy years—get in the practice of saving. Amen.

What's Your Investment Style?

This is so exciting, you guys. You get to start at the beginning. No regrets. Hopefully you have little to no debt.* *This is such an amazing time for you* and I am *so* jealous of your developing financial stylishness.

Three super general/starting-point investment style options:

- Conservative

- Moderate

- Aggressive

The financial field is bloated with terminology. We can't even begin to scale that mountain here, but we can start the discussion and plant a little seed that you can start tending, right? This is prime time to start thinking about this real-life application of everyone's favorite subject—*math.* These are just nuggets to chew on as you roll hard into managing your dollars.

How about some resources for you to use to dig deeper into investing styles and terminology:

- Thebalance.com

- Investopedia.com

- Sec.gov/investor

- Nerdwallet.com

- Parents, CPA, a respected friend, or a mentor; seek advice or recommendation for a good financial advisor

Popular Investment Strategies

An investment strategy is what guides the decisions of an investor based on goals, risk, and future capital needs. What is capital? It's the wealth, baby! There are stocks and bonds, cash, real estate, growth investment . . . there are terms like value, dividend, small cap, and growth.

Hello, microeconomics. This is where asking advice works to your advantage. Investing can be exhilarating, and it can be devastating. We'll be diving a bit into taxes in the next section, but make note: Don't forget about taxation on your investing adventures. It'll happen. You can always count on the tax guy to show up.

Gathering good information and asking advice from the right people are imperative. Here are some recommended places to start:

- *The Intelligent Investor* by Benjamin Graham—considered the bible of investing

- Dave Ramsey: Start at Daveramsey.com

- Forbes.com

- Mentors (remember chapter 9?) or get a referral to talk to a professional

---

* A note on debt, student loan debt to be specific: According to Credible. com, the current average student loan amount sits at $33,654, which averages out to a monthly loan payment of $393.

"For which of you, intending to build a tower, does not sit down first and count the cost, whether he has enough to finish it?"

—Luke 14:28

The idea of saving and or/investing can come with preconceived ideas. What are thoughts or fears or judgments you have about saving or investing? Considering the words in Luke 14:28, does that change your opinion at all? How? Or does it confirm what you already believe? If so . . . how?

_____

_____

_____

_____

_____

_____

_____

_____

_____

_____

_____

_____

_____

_____

Taxes, Man

"In this world nothing can be said to be certain,
except death and taxes."

—Benjamin Franklin

The tax man don't play. Even back in the biblical days, the struggle was real:

"Render therefore unto Caesar the things which are
Caesar's; and unto God the things that are God's."

—Matthew 22:21

Plan for taxes. Pay them. Prioritize them. Adulting is tough enough without the hammer of an IRS letter of delinquency (and the added interest and fees that come with it).

How Tax Brackets Work

Websites such as Taxfoundation.org, HRblock.com, and Bankrate.com keep an updated chart of federal tax brackets for the upcoming tax year. In short, individuals (and the array of marrieds or nots) are taxed a percentage of income depending on income amount. And depending on which state you live in, there could be state income tax, too. A quick Google search will return an answer pretty quick if you aren't already aware of state income tax where you live.

Self-Employment Taxes

Oh, boy. I think I just got an ulcer from typing that. My spouse and I have been in and out of self-employment for nearly our entire relationship. At first, we had *no idea* what we were doing.

Even just a tiny bit of research on self-employment tax liability could have saved us *years* of heartache (and debt).

The Social Security Administration (for the 2019 tax year) states, "If you work for an employer, you and your employer each pay a 6.2 percent Social Security tax on up to $132,900 of your earnings and a 1.45 percent Medicare tax on all earnings. *If you're self-employed, you pay the combined employee and employer amount, which is a 12.4 percent Social Security tax* on up to $132,900 of your net earnings and a 2.9 percent Medicare tax on your entire net earnings. If your earned income is more than $200,000 ($250,000 for married couples filing jointly), you must pay 0.9 percent more in Medicare taxes."

In the simplest terms: When an employee works for a company, the employer covers half of Social Security and Medicare tax, and when you're self-employed, *you* are responsible to pay the full amount.

Important: The company that pays you as a contractor pays *none of that,* which means:

- The check you received has no taxes removed to pay on your behalf.

- If you do not immediately tuck away, at the very, *very* least 15.3 percent for Social Security and Medicare, you will receive quite the wake-up call come April 15th.

It adds up *fast* and the IRS is neither merciful nor understanding.

And don't forget about state taxes for running a business, like B&O (business and operations), and probably even county and city business taxes.

A smart number to set aside for income and self-employment taxes from every freelance check: 30 percent. Some recommend 25 to 30 percent, but after a few intense dance-offs with the tax man, I don't like to risk it, so we shoot for 30 percent as often as we can. Of course, that number is somewhat fluid according to your income, so reference current tables for tax brackets.

If I could do it all over again, I would have hired a local CPA even before starting my own business.

Also related: Keep those receipts! Home office, software, hardware, mileage (this adds up, *track it—worth it!*), business-related meals and entertainment, even possibly a portion of utilities . . . a good CPA can help you maximize your deductions. I repeat: Save and log those receipts. Deductions are money you get to keep.

Write this five time below: Don't mess with the IRS. Or draw a picture of whatever you want. This topic *sucks*. Just get your wiggles out.

Full-Time Employee Taxes

With full-time employment, you can claim some allowances on the W4 tax form. The number of allowances you choose affects the taxes your employer deducts from your paycheck. The *more* allowances you claim, the *less* tax is withheld.

If you don't withhold enough, you can end up paying big come April 15th. If you have a lot withheld, that means an awesome tax return. But it's also money that could have been working for you all year (savings + interest). There are different methodologies surrounding this strategy. The fun news is: You get to choose your own path because yay adulting. (For more on this, see the document "If You Are Self-Employed" put out by the Social Security Administration at is www.ssa.gov/pubs/EN-05-10022.pdf.)

"Honour the LORD with thy substance, and with the firstfruits of all thine increase: So shall thy barns be filled with plenty, and thy presses shall burst out with new wine."

—*Proverbs 3:9–10*

Whew. Let's shake off the tax scaries with some dreaming. What dreams do you have? What do you want to be? How do you want to impact the world? How can a commitment to financial responsibility help you attain your goals and dreams?

_____

_____

_____

_____

_____

_____

_____

_____

_____

_____

_____

_____

_____

"And all that believed were together, and had all things common; And sold their possessions and goods, and parted them to all men, as every man had need. And they, continuing daily with one accord in the temple, and breaking bread from house to house, did eat their meat with gladness and singleness of heart, Praising God, and having favour with all the people. And the Lord added to the church daily such as should be saved."

—*Acts 2:44–47*

I am healthy, happy & capable. I am blessed with work & community.

I am fulfilled! I have been shown love and compassion... I have been lifted. Because I have been invested in, I am again able to support and help others.

I am not the only one who fulfills the words in Acts 2... I have been helped in my time of need.

What is this? I need help! Who will help me?

I see need and I take action.
There is lack or hurt in the
world/my community.
I am able to help!

I use my resources to
support, care for, and
encourage others in need.

I am fulfilled. It gives me joy
to help and meet needs. I am
grateful to have the privilege
of blessing and to be able to
use those blessings to help
others who lack or are in need.

Adulting means it's ALWAYS your turn to make dinner.
—Tami Stout
(actual adult)

Take to the Skies

Post-College

You've graduated. Now what?

On a practical level, there's the job hunt and the where-to-live situation. And there's the jury of family and/or public opinion who love to weigh in on life decisions.

We've touched on a lot of things in this book . . . from life skills to relationships and boundaries to purpose to career to finances . . . interwoven with much of the in between.

There has been advice, and there have been lots of questions. The purpose has been to introduce stuff you may not have begun to consider, but stuff that will play an important role now that your adulting is full speed ahead.

The hope is that when you close this book, you will feel at least 1 percent more prepared, and a lot percent more encouraged as you launch into your brave, new world.

The Bible was written and put together in a different lifetime, but isn't it amazing how God's word still applies to the lives we live today? Through scripture we find hope, we find promises, and we find inspirational instruction to help us along the way.

"For God, who commanded the light to shine out of darkness, hath shined in our hearts, to give the light of the knowledge of the glory of God in the face of Jesus Christ."

—2 Corinthians 4:6

It's easy to drop dope scripture and leave it like a mic drop, but that verse felt rather mic-drop-ish.

Faith and scripture don't guarantee an easy way. However, faith and scripture poured out and hidden in your amazing heart

(Psalms 119:11) lay a strong foundation as you explore and work to build a life on your own.

Whether you think you are or not, whether you fly or not, you *are* building a life. What kind of life are you building?

Post-Post College

Have you heard of this "extended adolescence"? In 2010 the *New York Times* ran a widely read article that brought this topic to the main stage . . . the idea that the range of adolescence is extending. Eighteen used to be the default "launch age," but it looks like that average number is moving more toward twenty-five.

I believe I see the trend, regardless of studies and data. But how does this affect you?

I can't answer that, but I do know that the chapters in this book were carefully crafted to give you information to process and chew on to get you to a solid launch pad. Opinion, trends, and scientific data are neither the aim nor the limit. As I wrote only paragraphs before:

> *Whether you think you are or not, you* are *building a life. What kind of life are you building?*

Your age is not your definition. There are some who will look down on your ~~flawless skin~~ youth, but scripture's got this on lockdown. "Let no man despise thy youth; but be thou an example of the believers, in word, in conversation, in charity, in spirit, in faith, in purity" (1 Timothy 4:12).

The folks who have been alive twice as long as you might look down on you, on your "youth." They may question your wisdom or skill. But 1 Timothy 4:12 encourages "be thou an example."

You have limitless potential and so much value to offer your job, community, family, and the world. You have a distinct, unique, amazing point of view, and take on creativity, regardless of your age. Really. But? This moment, this time in your life is tough. Being the young, inexperienced one, snuggled right up next to the pressure of becoming and establishing a life. That "limitless potential" sits in the seat right next to sooooooo many unknowns. Let's focus on what you have. Use the space below to list ways your "young adult-ness" is a benefit. What do these assets allow you to uniquely bring to the table?

"Put on therefore, as the elect of God, holy and beloved, bowels of mercies, kindness, humbleness of mind, meekness, longsuffering; Forbearing one another, and forgiving one another, if any man have a quarrel against any: even as Christ forgave you, so also do ye. And above all these things put on charity, which is the bond of perfectness. And let the peace of God rule in your hearts, to the which also ye are called in one body; and be ye thankful. Let the word of Christ dwell in you richly in all wisdom; teaching and admonishing one another in psalms and hymns and spiritual songs, singing with grace in your hearts to the LORD. And whatsoever ye do in word or deed, do all in the name of the Lord Jesus, giving thanks to God and the Father by him."

—Colossians 3:12-17

References

Bohanes, Michael. "'Following Your Passion' Is Dead. Here's What to Replace It With." *Forbes.* July 5, 2018.

Clear, James. *Atomic Habits.* Avery, 2018.

Cloud, Henry, and John Townsend. *Boundaries: When to Say Yes, How to Say No to Take Control of Your Life.* Zondervan, 1992.

Consumer.gov. "Your Credit History." Accessed November 26, 2019. https://www.consumer.gov/articles/1009-your-credit -history.

Credit Krama. "Buying a Car: How Much Can I afford?" October 23, 2019. https://www.creditkarma.com/auto/i/how -much-car-afford.

Eriksson, K., I. Vartanova, P. Strimling, and B. Simpson. "Generosity Pays: Selfish People Have Fewer Children and Earn Less Money." *Journal of Personality and Social Psychology.* 2018.

Fernández-Aráoz, Claudio. "Ignore Emotional Intelligence at Your Own Risk." *Harvard Business Journal.* October 22, 2014.

Fessler, Leah. "Selfish People Earn Less Money Than Generous People." *Quartz.* November 19, 2018.

Fiscal Fizzle. *"The Benefits of Renting: A Surprisingly Long List."* May 16, 2011. https://fiscalfizzle.com/2011/05/16/renting -benefits.

Graham, Benjamin. *The Intelligent Investor.* Harper Business, 1949.

Grant, Adam. *Give and Take: A Revolutionary Approach to Success.* Viking, 2013.

Goff, Bob. *Everybody, Always: Becoming Love in a World Full of Setbacks and Difficult People.* Thomas Nelson, 2018.

Haltiwanger, John. "The Science of Generosity: Why Giving Makes You So Happy." *Elite Daily.* December 24, 2014.

Hayes, Abby. "4 Things to Know When Buying Homeowners Insurance." *U.S. News & World Report.* February 14, 2014.

Hiller, Tim. *Strive: Life is Short, Pursue What Matters.* Deep River Books, 2015.

Investopedia. Accessed November 25, 2019. https://www .investopedia.com.

Kastner, Sabine, and Stephanie McMains. "Interactions of Top-Down and Bottom-Up Mechanisms in Human Visual Cortex." *The Journal of Neuroscience.* 2011 Jan 12; 31(2): 587–597.

Kerr, James. "6 Bad Things That Happen When Leaders Avoid Conflict." *Inc.* October 20, 2014.

King, Maxwell. *The Good Neighbor: The Life and Work of Fred Rogers.* Abrams, 2018.

Mayo Clinic. "Depression (Major Depressive Disorder)." Accessed November 26, 2019. https://www.mayoclinic.org /diseases-conditions/depression/symptoms-causes/syc -20356007.

McConnell, Allen R. "Giving Really Is Better Than Receiving." *Psychology Today.* December 25, 2010.

McDonald, Peter. *Oxford Dictionary of Medical Quotations.* Oxford University Press, 2004.

Post, Stephen G. "Altriusm, Happiness, and Health: It's Good to Be Good." *International Journal of Behavioral Medicine.* 2005 Jun; 12(2): 66–77.

Ramsey, Dave. "How Much Can I Afford?" Accessed November 25, 2019. https://www.daveramsey.com/blog/how-much -house-can-i-afford.

Reed, Philip. "How to Buy a New Car." *Nerd Wallet.* July 14, 2016.

Rose, Jeff. "The 5 Best Investment Strategies in a Volatile Market." *Forbes.* June 17, 2019.

Ryback, Ralph. "The Powerful Psychology Behind Cleanliness." *Psychology Today.* July 11, 2016.

Sethi, Ramit. "How to Negotiate Rent (to Save *Thousands* per Year)." *I Will Teach You To Be Rich.* October 8, 2019.

SocialSecurity.gov. "If You Are Self-Employed." Publication No. 05-10022. January 2019. https://www.ssa.gov/pubs/EN-05 -10022.pdf.

Stetka, Bret. "Extended Adolescence: When 25 Is the New 18." *Scientific American.* September 19, 2017.

Weiss, R. J. "Dave Ramsey Recommended Household Budget Percentages (+How to Determine Your Own)." *The Ways To Wealth.* October 17, 2019.

Wells Fargo Debt-to-Income Ratio Calculator. Accessed November 26, 2019. https://www.wellsfargo.com/goals-credit /debt-to-income-calculator.

Verse Index

Index

Acknowledgments

To my mom and dad, thank you for your example of enduring faith, and for working tirelessly to provide the resources and wings needed to not only make it but to fly.

To my younger and taller sister and brother . . . I'm not jealous. OK, I am, but I love you both anyway.

To my in-laws, for lovingly folding me into this crazy, wonderful family.

To Casey Peterson, Kerry Kearney, Lisa Gsellman, and Sara Wood . . . I strongly credit my one lasting thread of sanity through two decades of motherhood to the consistent support of these women.

To my IRL "village"—the ones I coffee with, volunteer with, exercise with, church with, watch school sports with, text with, happy hour with . . . as we watch our "babies" launch and leave our nests [sob]. Thank you for lovingly building the village in which we raise our families. You all inspire me.

To Morgan Shanahan, my dynamic, supportive editor who had the courage to trust little ol' me with this big ol' idea.

To the AFs (they know who they are), and my great, big extended blogging family. They give and cheer and lift and connect and actively seek ways to help each other succeed. This book is a result of that lifting and giving.

To Mr. Langworthy. The BEST ENGLISH TEACHER EVER. Your reflection of God's faithful heart and belief in a girl who couldn't see much in herself made an immeasurable, beautiful impact on the trajectory of my life.

To my kids, Joel, Olivia, and Lucy. Thank you for your genuine excitement when I try new things, and for enduring my many words when fewer would be better [wink]. Y'all are a total blast and make me so, so proud to be your mom.

To my husband, my partner in dreaming. You help move the clouds to let the sunshine in. Thank you for your relentless support and love.

To God, for He has woven a beautiful tapestry of community. I thank Him for the ups and downs that have created the path that has lead to here. "For I know the plans I have for you," declares the Lord, "plans to prosper you and not to harm you, plans to give you hope and a future." (Jeremiah 29:11)... Amen.

About the Author

Jenny is a well-caffeinated mother of three grown-ish and almost grown "kids" who consumes gallons of coffee in the Pacific Northwest with her husband of 25+ years. Since 2004, she has authored the popular blog *Jenny on the Spot* a parenting, lifestyle, and humor-centered blog featuring the occasional craft and recipe ... because that's what the people want. Her work and writing have been featured in such places as Huffington Post, BuzzFeed,  *Redbook, Parents Magazine*, Blog Design for Dummies, local media outlets, and has likely made it into a few of her kids' Snaps and/or nightmares.

Jenny is a former secondary school teacher turned stay-at-home mom turned work-at-home mom. Over much of the last 25 years, Jenny and her husband, Paul, have adopted the lifestyle of relentless entrepreneurs. This book is another artery connecting to that entrepreneurial heart. Plus, she's a mom ... so she loves any opportunity to tell people how to do stuff. Learn more about Jenny at jennyonthespot.com, on Instagram at @jennyonthespot, or Facebook.com/thejennyonthespot.